Hush

The Second Installment in the Chloe Daniels Mysteries

By

Deidra D. S. Green

HUSH

Copyright 2016 Deidra D. S. Green

RATHSI Publishing, LLC

www.rathsipublishing.com

ISBN#: 978-0-9977168-7-0

Printed in the United States of America

Other Books by Deidra D. S. Green:

- Sick, Sicker, Sickest (The first installment in the Chloe Daniels Mysteries)
- Twisted Sister
- Twisted Sister II: Twisted's Revenge

- Twisted Sister III: After the Twist
- TRENT
- Woman at the Top of the Stairs
- Woman at the Top of the Stairs II: Sweetest Revenge
- Woman at the Top of the Stairs III: The Final Say
- A Letter to My Mother (Four Part Letter Series)
- Elite Affairs: Orchestrated Beauty
- Elite Affairs II: Simple Elegance
- Suddenly Single: So Undeserving
- Let the Church Say
- Ivy: Some Say she's Poison
- My Guy Friday
- They Call Me Ms. Cleo (Miss Dee)
- Interstate 64

Visit Deidra D. S. Green at http://deidrawrites.weebly.com/

Read Deidra's Blog at http://deidrawrites.weebly.com/

Follow Deidra on Twitter- @deidrag

Follow Deidra on Instagram @deidra_d.s._green

**Subscribe to Deidra's newsletter here: Free Read when you sign up for my newsletter :) :) https://www.instafreebie.com/free/Vev7x

**For those who would like to purchase paperback copies, feel free to shop at Deidra's store: http://www.store10888205.ecwid.com

Join Deidra on FB at http://www.facebook.com/deidra.d.green

Acknowledgements

Anna Black is back!

I have to start by saying Thank you so much for your patience. I know this sequel has been a long time coming but I hope you will find that it is more than worth the wait!

Giving honor to the Creator for giving me life and blessing me with the love of the written word. Thank you to my publishing company, our family business, Rathsi Publishing. Thanks to my graphic designer, Lashawone for helping me to reimagine and recreate a cover designed some three years ago. Lashawone, I want you to know I appreciate how hard you work on my behalf, how tirelessly you work in support of this dream of mine. I will never take your talent, support, patience or hard work for granted. Thank you, thank you and thank you to my reading family. You hall have been rocking with me for years and this wouldn't be nearly as much fun without you.

I have to give a special Thank You shout out to Heaven Daria Rain. When I thought no one cared about Anna Black and her crazy antics, Heaven was the one who reminded me that there were people who love Anna like I do and wanted to see the story move forward. That day, When Heaven reached out to me on social media, I went to my archives and found this story. It had been sitting dormant for nearly a year. I dusted it off and fell in love with the characters all over again. So, Heaven, please know that I appreciate you. I appreciate you breathing life back into this series and I appreciate you giving me the push I needed. Thank you so much!

To my family and dear friends, I appreciate the support. To my beloved children, VcToryann C'Mone and Kamerron DeAnthony Alexander, all I do is for you.

Dedication

This one is dedicated to you, my reading family. Thanks for continuing to hold me down...

 # Chapter One

A new body...

Those words were always disturbing but particularly in this situation. The Atlanta Metropolitan Police Department called Dr. Chloe Daniels in because they had a case completely confounding them. This new body would be added to the two bodies the police didn't want to admit were connected. Dr. Daniels had, up until this point, reserved judgment in linking the bodies. Considering what Addison, her partner for the past three years was saying about the newest victim, there may well be a connection; a connection that would mean there was a new serial killer in Atlanta.

"The victim is a black woman, they think in her late 20's maybe early 30's. She was found under an overpass, fully dressed, and fully made up. The clothes were just like the one's we'd seen before, frilly and childlike. We won't know how long she's been deceased until we get on scene. The medical examiner should be there by now."

Addison was good at the details; helping to keep Chloe abreast of new developments, appointments, and her tedious schedule. Addison had been a great addition but Chloe knew there was more she wanted to say. After a few minutes of silence, as the two women moved through Atlanta traffic, Addison spoke again.

"I know the police have reservations but this one fits the bill... classic for the baby doll killer," Addison added.

"So that's what we're calling the murderer now?"

Chloe had to laugh. She hated the monikers people couldn't resist giving serial killers. At this point, she was completely convinced they had one whether the police and particularly Chief Blake Livingston believed it to be true or not. Acknowledging a serial killer was a double edged sword. The public would of course be notified of the impending threat causing hyper-awareness, but also greater precaution. At the same time, the killer, being acknowledged by the public and in the media, might escalate the kills in order to maintain relevance in the public's eye. Many of the one's Dr. Daniels encountered in the past were attention whore's, thrilled just as much from the attention as they were from the killing itself.

Traffic slowed to a crawl on Interstate 85, not far from the Capitol building. Stagnant traffic in downtown Atlanta was typical; however, Chloe knew this particular traffic jam was a direct result of the crime scene less than a mile ahead. Swirling red and blue lights dotted their approach as they pulled closer in. A few officers decked in eerily yellow fluorescing vests atop their midnight blue uniforms guided traffic away from the yellow and black tape draped slightly above bright orange traffic cones. One officer, noting their approach, waved them in near the other official vehicles. Addison eased the black SUV over to the cornered off area immediately under the overpass just outside the yellow tape. Addison exited the driver's side making sure to grab everything Dr. Daniels could possibly need to inspect the scene. After flashing her credentials, Chloe Daniels breached the yellow tape with Addison just a few feet behind her.

Just like Atlanta traffic was common, so was the attention Dr. Chloe Daniels attracted when entering a crime scene. This crime scene was no different. Most if not all of the police officers on site were men and they undoubtedly noted the doctor's presence. If there were women present it was hard to tell because of the dark uniform, police cap with hair neatly tucked underneath, and standard-issue hardware. The exact opposite was true for Chloe. Her natural good looks were not restrained by masculinized clothing and nondescript uniformity. Standing five eight, Chloe's café ole' skin, curvaceous figure and confident air provided the male officers a pleasant distraction and the female officers a reason to try and flaunt their femininity. Addison offered a very different presentation. She too was beautiful but her caramel skin and dark brooding eyes were hidden behind large rimmed eyeglasses. Addison's natural curly hair was pulled back tight in a bun and her womanly curves were cloaked with dark oversized clothing.

Lead detective, Michael Phillips made his way over to the attractive psychologist. Detective Phillips kept a straight face, determined to keep things professional. He'd had a thing for Chloe ever since his boss, Chief of Police Blake Livingston, introduced them more than a year and a half ago. Without question, he was immediately attracted to her good looks. Once he worked the first case with her, Michael became enchanted with her cool wit, sophistication and intelligence. Working late nights on the case drew the two closer together professionally but Michael wanted much more than that. He'd made some subtle advances but his passive ways went virtually unnoticed, at least as far as he could tell. Michael was undeterred. He was more determined than ever to get to know Chloe intimately. Today he would keep to the script... business... strictly business.

"Doctor."

"Detective."

Their greetings were courteous yet trite.

"The body's over here."

Dr. Daniels followed in Detective Michael's footsteps with Addison in tow. The silence around Chloe increased with every step she took. Everything around her was summarily blocked out as she zoned in on the body. Movement ceased and conversation faded into the background. Traffic behind her disintegrated into nothingness. The yellow tape disappeared. Police officers milling around were frozen in time. It was just her and the cognitive processes necessary to thoroughly assess what lay before her.

The ornate and brightly colored clothes on the body stood as a stark contrast against the mundane coloring of the concrete backdrop. On an adult size body, the clothes were almost cartoonish; bright red-smock like shirt with an oversized rounded ruffle collar and matching knickers with scalloped trim on the bottom. The knickers stopped mid-calf. Chloe scanned the length of the victim's legs. There were obvious abrasions and scratches, some fresh and some scabbed over. White lacy ankle socks led to shiny black patent leather shoes. As Chloe moved down for closer inspection, it appeared the shoes were forced on like they were too little for the intended victim. The woman was fully made up as Addison described but the applied makeup didn't appear designed to accentuate the victims' features. Rather, it seemed whoever did the cosmetic application intended to mock the victim. Chloe squatted down to get a closer look. The mild wind stirred around the undeniable smell of death.

The victim lay perfectly still; her dead eyes standing wide open. Leaning in closer, Chloe could see that the victims' black pupils were offset by pronounced reddish swollen veins bulging in the stark whiteness of her eyes. Mascara had been recklessly applied with thick clumps of hardened black liquid weighing down the victim's eyelids. Cobalt blue eyeshadow encircled the dead woman's eyes. Heavy was not the word to describe it. Layers upon layers of shadow had been packed onto the eyelid; enough to make the youth in the lid appear old and heavy. The coloring extended far beyond the victim's eyes, bleeding into her hairline. Pearly white eye shadow highlights accentuated the blue underneath. It was just as thick and carelessly applied. Her skin was ashen due to the lack of life-giving blood circulating through her veins. Rounded circles of hot pink blush traced the victims' now sunken cheeks. Messy ruby red lipstick covered her mouth pass the victim's natural lip line, exaggerating the pout of her lips.

Chloe stood to her feet having fully examined the body. She moved closer to the victim's head and stood over the body sprawled on the asphalt pavement. It was a risky move for the killer, leaving the body right out in the open. Considering the almost constant flow of traffic down interstate 85, the perpetrator had to be confident, possibly overconfident of not getting caught dumping the corpse. The vehicle had to be big enough and the dump had to be executed swift enough to not draw unwarranted attention. Flashes of light brought Dr. Daniels out of her self-induced solitude.

"Any identification on the body?" Dr. Daniels asked.

"No."

"Cause of death?" she inquired.

"Strangulation."

Detective Phillips came back into her purview. He knelt down and with latex covered hands pulled back the ruffling on the collar to reveal ligature marks. Chloe crouched down next to him, their bodies nearly touching, to take a closer look. Phillips inhaled drawing in her sultrily scented perfume. For the briefest moment, he imagined they were somewhere else; somewhere less deadly. Chloe extended her hand and Addison placed latex gloves in them. After gloving up, Dr. Daniels eased the collar back a bit more, noticing the variation in the depth and width of the strangulation marks.

"Any indication of the weapon of choice?"

"It's hard to tell," offered Detective Phillips. "The abrasions are inconsistent and if you look real close, the marks seem porous – not like a belt or even a rope."

Porous... Chloe made another mental note. More flashes of incandescent light.

The two stood up simultaneously.

"You still think there's no connection?" Chloe's question reeked of 'I told you so'.

"It's not me who doesn't want to admit it and he wants us both to report to headquarters immediately."

Detective Phillips didn't need to say anything more. Chloe knew who the 'he' was. Releasing her hands from the binding latex gloves and handing them back to Addison, Chloe checked her watch.

"Do I have time for this?"

"Yes, we've got a few hours before our next appointment," Addison replied pocketing the gloves.

"Tell the chief I will meet with him but I want in on the autopsy."

"No problem. Meet you there in 15."

Doctor Daniels and Detective Phillips temporarily parted ways. Dr. Daniels and her assistant made their way under the yellow tape and through the local news crews that had gathered.

"Dr. Daniels, Dr. Daniels, would you care to make a statement?"

"Dr. Daniels... Dr. Daniels?"

She knew better than to feed the hungry natives.

"No comment."

They followed behind her. Chloe ignored them.

Addison shunned the cameras altogether. They continued to flash as Addison took her position in the driver's seat and started up the SUV. Chloe took off her steel gray pin-striped suit jacket and laid it over the backseat before climbing into the truck. Her crisp white blouse stayed tucked neatly in the top of her slacks. She rolled down the windows to relieve the warmth and erase any trace evidence of death lingering.

Thomasville Georgia – teetering on the very edge of southwest Georgia. Population 18,000. That was Anna Black's newest location after absconding from Atlanta. Thomasville was small town Georgia with small town ways; disconnected in time and distance from the bustling metropolis Anna had no choice but to abandon. She'd watched the small screen in the cheap hotel room that was her momentary hideout; the news people talking about her as though she were an abomination, a demon set out to hurt the innocent. They didn't understand that she was just the opposite of that. She was an angel.

So much had changed about her, not just her location but her appearance. She was no longer a shoulder length brunette. Anna's hair was now shorter and platinum blonde. Although Anna intended to cut it much shorter, she hesitated, desiring to still feel like her previous self. That may have been a dangerous proposition but Anna couldn't completely separate with who she was. At the same time, Anna couldn't run the risk of disconnected Thomasville being connected enough to learn of her past. She took her mother's maiden name, Montgomery and built a profile suitable enough to shake the leeches from her trail. Yes, some things changed, but Anna's mission stayed strong.

Anna already planned to leave her parents' home. She didn't plan on having to run for her life from the hospital and city she loved so much. With the monies she'd saved up and a bit of finagling, Anna was able to find a small room in a boarding home. The woman who ran the home was old and fortunately out of touch with Anna's reality. People in Thomasville didn't know about her past. The news of Atlanta wasn't necessarily the news of Anna's new residence. It would be temporary. Anna knew that going in. But she needed time; time to get the necessary licensure to practice as an LPN in her future location – Florida. The city wouldn't matter nearly as much as getting her credentials in order. That was her second priority. The first she'd already resolved by finding work.

Chapter Two

Her sleep was disturbed. Finding rest proved more and more difficult. The vision she so desperately sought to eliminate had been burned into her memory and she couldn't shake it. The sounds... the visual... the betrayal kept her from resting. Her subconscious mind fought against the pained memories attempting to shut them down even in slumber. There was no success to be had. She continued to be haunted.

That day was just like any other day. Her husband, a successful financial consultant left the house early for work. Her two children were at school and she'd taken the opportunity for a little girl time. Retail therapy before a few sets of tennis at the country club was just what the doctor ordered. By the time she got home, all Grace Pembroke Wetherby could think about was taking a nice hot shower. Pulling her car into their three-car garage, Grace noticed her husband's car in its customary spot. She was sure when she left out earlier his car was gone. Maybe he'd forgotten something and had to come back, she thought to herself, entering the home. She stopped just long enough to grab a bottle of water out of the refrigerator before bounding up the stairs to the master suite. Getting in a steaming shower would be the last of her "me" time as the children would be home soon and she would quickly be swept back into mommy and wife mode.

The door to their bedroom was closed. Grace found that odd considering the only time they'd close the door is if she and her husband were handling adult business. The thought prevented her from hearing the moans coming from inside the suite. Grace's hesitation was only brief as she opened the bedroom door. Their reaction is what made her focus on something other than the shower. It took Grace a minute to process what she was seeing; her mind desperately wanting to deny what her eyes revealed. The girls' black ashy legs were thrown across his pale white shoulders and he was in mid thrust. What had been saved solely for her was being shared with the help... the fuckin' help... This scene played over and over in Grace's mind. Her subconscious tried to squelch it even in her sleep but the memory was too vivid to be denied.

Drake pushed the girl's legs down and crawled out of the bed; his wood still standing at full mast. He clumsily grabbed his shorts lying nearby. Grace could only stand there, not blinking, refusing to think. The girl recoiled turning away from him. For the briefest moment, her eyes met those of the woman whose husband she just screwed. The girl climbed out of the bed with Grace's high count sheet wrapped around her. Both advanced towards Grace at the same time; both with different intentions.

"Drop it," Grace scowled, pointing at the girl. There was no thought of protestation as the look in her boss' eyes said it all. The girl did as she was told dropping the sheet; using her hands to cover her feminine parts. Embarrassed, the girl lowered her head and made steps towards exiting the door.

Before she could clear the threshold, she felt hot stings to her tender flesh.

"You lousy fuckin coon bitch! How dare you!" The blows continued to fly until they were stopped by Grace's husband. Grace didn't stop flailing, instead landing her frustrated blows to the chest of her husband, giving the girl the opportunity to escape. Her clothes were still in the room but there was no time to grab them. The help traversed the stairs. She'd find something to cover her nakedness. Grace's fury blazed and comingled with pained tears that stung her eyes.

"Don't touch me! How could you do that to me? Get away from me!"

Drake took every blow she dished out and every foul word she uttered. Grabbing her hands he pulled his wife into him as much holding her as ending the physical assault. Although she was pinned, it didn't stop Grace from letting him know exactly what she thought of him.

"Let me go you fuckin bastard... you smell like nigger..."

Her breath was hot and venomous against his bare chest. Grace bucked against him, still trying to physically hurt him as much as he'd hurt her. Drake held her tighter and tried to explain. She cursed him again. She squirmed and kicked. Drake had no choice but to release her. No words he said could quail the plethora of emotions she felt. The arms previously holding her dropped and with it his pride. Grace moved robotically toward the shower. The water, turned to maximum heat, quickly steamed the glass enclosure and encompassed the footprint of the expansive bathroom. She methodically peeled off her clothes dropping them onto the travertine floor. Grace stepped into the shower; the boiling pearls of water fiercely indenting her alabaster skin. She didn't flinch taking all the painful pricks the shower had to offer. Her tears now comingled with the water from overhead. Grace vowed at that very moment to get revenge. That's where the dream stopped and her quest to right his wrongs began.

226 Peachtree Street SW was just about as busy as any Atlanta tourist attraction. Addison and Chloe used their police business signage to snag a parking spot and made their way into the building. Chloe knew exactly where to go. She'd met with the chief numerous times before. Those meetings hadn't always been pleasant. She didn't expect this one to be either. Addison took up residence immediately outside the Chief's office. His secretary let Chloe in.

"You summoned?" Chloe quipped.

"Good to see you too, Dr. Daniels. Please take a seat," Chief Blake Livingston replied. He was a distinguished looking man; the hard lines creasing his pecan complexion representative of too many years in the field. Gray hair around his temples was from too much worry and stress gained from his years behind the desk. There was a soft rap at the door and Detective Phillips entered. Chloe didn't have to turn around to know he was in the room.

"Sorry boss gotta little hung up."

"Just have a seat detective so we can get this thing done." The Chief sounded irritated. Phillips took up the seat next to Chloe. Chief Livingston was brooding, looking back and forth between the two of them.

"Three bodies in a little less than four months. Almost two months between the first and second victim and now in less than three weeks we have a third body. The body count is growing and the kills are coming closer together." The Chief was extrapolating but not to either one of them in particular.

"So you're acknowledging that the cases are connected?" Chloe crossed her legs and swung her crimson red stilettoed foot in the air.

The lines in the Chiefs' face deepened. He didn't want to admit it. Murder by a serial killer brought on a whole new echelon of scrutiny from his supervisors and a whole new level of angst for the people of his city. Livingston put his elbows on his desk amidst stacks of files and papers and rubbed his temples.

"We had press on the scene." Detective Phillips knew the information wouldn't help the Chief feel any better but he needed to know.

"Fuck! That's just what we needed." The Chief took another elongated moment before responding further.

"To answer your question Dr. Daniels, I have no choice but to believe we do indeed have a serial killer on our hands. We have to get ahead of this one."

"We're already behind," Chloe reminded the Chief. "You can be sure the media will be headlining the story and will suggest the connection."

There had been some press at the first drop site because of the public location. More turned up at the second one and this time every major news station in the area had a camera crew present.

Reporters offered commentary on site. The police were definitely not ahead of the story.

"I need every available homicide officer combing the streets. We have got to find this killer and quick. I want you guys on this thing around the clock, do you understand detective, around the fuckin' clock. No one sleeps, no one eats, no one so much as takes a shit... you understand me?"

"Yes sir." Detective Phillips knew he was being dismissed and hurriedly exited the room. As lead on this case, he had to make sure the Chief's orders were followed to the letter. After hearing the door securely closed, Chief Livingston leaned in.

"I need you on this, more than ever."

Chloe and the Chief had an interesting relationship. It was love/hate and they both recognized it for what it was. In the beginning, Livingston discounted the benefit of having behavioral analysis used with any of his cases. He thought it all to be psycho mumbo jumbo. But Dr. Daniels had proven herself. The Chief hated to admit it but she had helped him out in the past.

With no clear leads on this case, he needed all the help he could get, psycho-babble or not.

"Unrestricted access... no red tape. Those are my conditions." Chloe uncrossed her legs and leaned in, closing the distance between herself and the Chief.

"Done." It was a compromise he was willing to make.

"And my fee?" Dr. Daniels smiled coyly. "Doubled..."

Chief Livingston nodded his head.

He stood to his feet and Chloe followed in kind. The two shook hands and Chloe turned to leave the office.

"Call me when the medical examiner is ready." She didn't wait for a response and made her exit. Seeing her boss on the move, Addison got up and moved in step with her.

"Contact Phillips. I need copies of the case files from the earlier victims."

"Got it." Addison was dialing before they exited the building.

Anna wanted to call her parents, to tell them the news people were wrong about her, but that would be risky. Anna's real motivation for calling would be to see if her parents really cared, whether they were paying attention now... However, Anna could only contemplate her parents' attentiveness for a little while. She had to handle business, the first of which was meeting with her new clients. As Anna Montgomery, fake credentials and all, was able to get on board the small local hospital, John D. Archibald. They were desperate for highly qualified staff who would be willing to work late nights and weekends. With Anna's stellar resume, they hired her almost instantaneously. Of course, at some point they would run background and find out that Anna Montgomery didn't really exist, but by that time. it would be far too late. Anna would have moved on to greener pastures and taken a few unsuspecting patients with her.

John D. Archibald Memorial Hospital was very different than Grady Hospital in Atlanta. Grady was a level one trauma center. Archibald was not. The pace was much slower and the patient size was much smaller. Anna could not wait to familiarize herself with the neediest patients. Head Nurse Blanche Stanley took it upon herself to show her new charge around the small but community oriented hospital.

"I know our little corner of the world is not as fancy as where you are from, but we get along alright," Nurse Stanley began.

Anna kept up with her stride for stride. She was glad to be dressed once again in her pressed whites. Despite the distance, being back in uniform was home for Anna. The tour continued.

"Once a month on the first Thursday afternoon from one to six p.m. we hold a free clinic."

"Free," Anna inquired.

"Yes," Nurse Stanley continued. "A lot of our locals don't have the best health care coverage or no insurance at all. We do the free clinic so they can at least get a check-up, tend to an emergency, broken bones and such no major surgery, and vaccinations."

Anna smiled at the notion of the thoughtfulness of such a gesture, but her primary interest began to show.

"Do you all have an intensive care unit?"

Nurse Stanley turned another corner and proceeded to respond.

"No, nothing like that. For our more serious patients, we try and stabilize them as best we can here. Then, we send them to the bigger hospitals. Grady is one of the sites we use if they are especially critical."

"What about geriatrics or neonatal care?"

Anna loved the babies and the elderly. You can tell a lot about a community by the way they take care of these two particular populations her daddy always said.

"We do have a small section of the hospital for the terminally ill, if that's what you mean," Nurse Stanley replied. "Our maternity ward is sufficient. As long as the babies are born healthy they stay the regular two to three days before being discharged with their mother. But if anyone is in serious medical need, and require highly specialized care, we send them where they can best be served."

The tour continued. The people they passed in the hallways were friendly. Everybody spoke like they had known you all their lives. Anna took special note of the location of the small pharmacy distribution closet as well as the geriatric wing. As the duo neared their return to the primary nurses' station, they were approached by a fellow nurse.

"Just in time," Nurse Stanley began. "Nurse Montgomery, this is Nurse Sophie Lynn Drysdale, Sophie Lynn for short." The two nurses exchanged pleasant greetings. "Nurse Drysdale will be responsible for getting you fully acclimated to our set-up. You will shadow her for this evenings shift and tomorrow, you will shadow her half shift and be on your own. Any questions?"

"No ma'am that sounds just fine," Anna offered with a fake smile.

"Good then. I have some paperwork to finish up before my shift is over so I will see you ladies later."

Anna and Sophia Lynn watched briefly as Nurse Stanley made her exit.

"We can start with rounds," Nurse Drysdale began, reaching onto the counter and retrieving the notes from the earlier shift. Nurse Drysdale seemed very matter of fact to be as young looking as she appeared, Anna surmised.

"I really appreciate you taking out the time to let me follow you around," Anna offered, feigning greater interest than was true to her character.

"No problem," Sophie Lynn replied dryly. "We all have to start somewhere.

Nurse Drysdale took a right from the nursing station and moved to the furthest end of the adjoining hallway.

"I like to start this way, work back to the nursing station. Cuts down on some of the walking," she offered. "Lord knows after ten years of twelve hour shifts on your feet, saving a few steps is worth it."

"Good afternoon Mr. Clark," Nurse Drysdale said as she entered the patient's room. "Mr. Dunn, how are you two feeling today?"

"Oh, as well as can be expected," the man closest to the door replied. The man furthest away looked at the two nurses, grunted and rolled over.

"Gallstone surgery for this one," Nurse Drysdale said as she perused the chart at the end of the bed. "You're looking well Mr. Clark. We should be able to let you go home tomorrow."

"You don't have to rush me out," the gentleman replied. "I like having all these young women around taking care of me. No need to rush at all." The man smiled widely, showing off a few missing teeth.

"I don't know if your wife would appreciate that now, Mr. Clark," Nurse Drysdale chastised. She seemed much more pleasant with the patients than she did one on one.

"When the cat's away, this old mouse will play."

Mr. Clark laughed at his own joke, to the point that he nearly choked himself. He started hacking and coughing. Anna was quick to pour him a glass of water from the bedside table. He took the glass in his wrinkly hand and when the coughing subsided, took a big gulp.

"Whew, that sure did make my incision hurt," the patient said, grabbing on to his side with his free hand.

"Now, now, if you promise to be good, I will send Nurse Black back with something for the pain. No more joking around for you, okay?"

Mr. Clark nodded his head and took another sip of water. Over the rim of the glass, he watched the two move to the next patient. He did like seeing all the pretty young ladies milling about. That he would certainly miss when he returned home to his double wide trailer and his equally wide wife.

The next patient was not nearly as excited to see the nurses. His back was still to them as they approached.

"Mr. Dunn," Nurse Sophie Lynn said, trying to get his attention.

Mr. Dunn responded by pulling the covers up almost completely covering his head. Nurse

Sophie was not dissuaded. She checked the doctor's notes on the chart and then proceeded to the side of the bed to check the heart monitor attached to him. Anna moved to a position where she could see the machine's readings. His vitals were stable with the exception of an increase in heart rate; not a dangerous increase, but an elevation nonetheless.

"Triple bypass surgery about two months ago at one of the bigger hospitals. He's been here with us for the past week or so for monitoring."

"How's he doing?"

When Nurse Drysdale spoke this time, she responded louder. Mr. Dunn had no choice but to hear her.

"If he would stop being so dang stubborn, he could leave."

There was a beeping notification on the monitor indicating a spike in heart rate.

"Now, I'm gonna need you to calm down Mr. Dunn. No need in getting all riled up, even if you are under the cover."

Mr. Dunn must have listened to all he cared to. Throwing the covers nearly off the bed, he sat straight up with a scowl on his face scary enough to frighten a small child.

"If you would just leave me the hell alone my heart would be fine."

Anna covered her mouth to hide a smile. Instead of being threatening, Mr. Dunn was actually kind of funny. Nurse Sophie Lynn didn't echo Anna's sentiment.

"Do you hear that machine Mr. Dunn? It says you are bordering on the verge of another heart attack if you don't calm down. Now, we're gonna leave and I expect you to lay in that bed, practice some deep breathing and pull yourself together. I will be back to check on you in exactly one hour and I expect your heart rate to be back to normal!"

Nurse Drysdale chastised him like a tantrumming child and he responded the same way; grabbing up his covers and throwing himself back down on the bed. Mr. Dunn turned over on his side and didn't utter another word. Satisfied that her patient got the message, Sophie Lynn proceeded to exit the room. Anna looked back at Mr. Dunn with a smile. He was at the top of her list of patients who could use her help. But rounds were just getting started. Anna hoped that a better candidate would soon emerge. She eagerly followed Nurse Sophie Lynn to the next room.

The doorbell rang. Grace Pembroke Wetherby was ready for the next interview. She crossed the Brazilian hardwood floors of her living room and entered the high polished marble floored two-story entry way. Smoothing down her pastel floral-print A-line dress, she opened the heavy glass and iron door.

"Mrs. Wetherby?" The young woman standing before her asked.

Grace sized her up, tracing her stature from the top of her nappy head to the soles of her feet.

The smile she offered the young woman was deceivingly pleasant.

"Yes, please come in."

Mrs. Wetherby allowed the young woman to pass her before moving behind and closing the oversized rod iron and glass door.

"Follow me."

The young woman did as she was told and followed Mrs. Wetherby down the expansive hallway and into the kitchen near the back of the home. She waited until invited to sit. Mrs. Wetherby took note of that. Her prepared list of questions was on the table along with a pen. After sitting at the head of the dinette table and pointing to a side chair for the guest to sit in, Grace began.

"Your name again? Tangerine, Orangutan?"

"No ma'am, Tangela... my name is Tangela Smith."

Grace snickered mockingly. She figured the girl was too dumb to know she was making fun of her.

"Oh my," Grace continued. "Moving on...age?"

"19."

"Have you ever worked as a nanny before? You are rather young." Grace's gaze was unwavering and judgmental. Any semblance of humor or lightheartedness was gone.

"Not directly as a nanny but I have worked at a daycare in the summers to earn money for college."

"Ummph..." Grace made notes and smiled deviously nonetheless.

"How old are your children, if you don't mind me asking," Tangela inquired.

It really wasn't her business since the girl would barely have a chance to care for them. Of course, Grace did mind but she answered anyway, not wanting to frighten the girl off.

"They are eight and six, both in school. That's why, if I decide to hire you, your work would be comprised of house cleaning and caring for them during the after school hours primarily."

"Oh that would work well with my school schedule, I mean, if you did decide I was the best fit."

If you only knew you nigger bitch.

Grace kept those sentiments to herself. She didn't want to have the girl in her house too long so she wrapped up the interview."

Well, Tanquilla," Grace said, exaggerating each syllable, "I have all the information I need."

Mrs. Wetherby got up from her chair and started back down the hall towards the front door. She didn't wait for the girl to follow her but expected that she would. Grace had the door opened before Tangela caught up with her.

"How soon can you start?"

"Really, I got the job?" Tangela's excitement showed.

"That depends. How soon can you start?"

"I can be here first thing tomorrow."

"Make first thing 6:30. That's a.m."

As soon as Tangela crossed the threshold of the door and before she could thank her new employer, Mrs. Wetherby closed the door; the rod iron tingling as the door settled into the closed and locked position. Tangela bounded down the front stairs. She couldn't be more excited about her new job.

Grace made her way to the library just off the living room. It was one of her favorite places in her million dollar home. Pouring brandy from a snifter, Grace took a hefty sip before sitting down in one of the oversized leather chairs. Her father's words danced around in her head. "Jigaboos ain't good but for a couple of things and shucking and jiving is one of them." She had to laugh at her father's colorful language. Yes, Tangela was the perfect fit. Grace couldn't wait to see how well she danced.

Chapter Three

It was the wee hours of the morning. After the meeting with the chief and the prosecuting attorney on the Anna Black case, Chloe Daniels day was still not over. They'd received the files from Phillips and dissected the information. Addison left around midnight. Chloe took a hot shower and changed into lounging clothes; a comfortable pair of sweat pants and a tank top. Returning to the office established in her home, Chloe continued pouring over the files Detective Phillips messengered over. Chloe sipped a crisp sauvignon blanc as she cross checked the details.

All three of the victims were young black females.

All three were found under overpasses on major highways in and around downtown Atlanta. A very bold move on the part of the killer.

Post-mortem rigidity had set in with all three bodies. They were found within 24 to 48 hours after they were murdered.

All three were found with clothes on better suited for a doll baby than an adult woman.

The clown-like makeup was consistent between the victims.

Strangulation was the cause of death for the first two and Chloe was sure it would be the same for victim number three. Her assumption she expected to soon be confirmed by the autopsy she would attend.

Missing person's reports in Atlanta had been raked over for the first two victims and there was no hit.

No murder weapon... no DNA evidence...

None of the crime scenes to date gave any indication as to whether the perpetrator was a man or woman, black, white or other. What was the motive? That was the question Chloe kept asking herself as she scoured every available detail. The previously full bottle of sauvignon was now half empty. Chloe nibbled on a bit of cold cheese pizza as she contemplated. There had to be clues to help identify the killer somewhere. They just hadn't been found yet. It would be hard to develop a real profile for the perpetrator without anything to go on. Chief Livingston was counting on that profile. Maybe the clue was in the costumes themselves. Chloe needed to get her hands on the clothes. That would be her first priority after meeting with the medical examiner at nine a.m.

Dr. Daniels wasn't the only one burning the midnight oil. Detective Phillips, sitting on his couch dressed in a t-shirt and cut off sweat pants, was also hard at work. He had copies of the files as well, going over the crime scenes trying to see something he may have missed before. The crimes didn't make sense to him. Sure they were connected and he was fairly certain the same perpetrator was responsible for all three but why? Every murderer had a motive, an end they were trying to achieve. What was the end for this killer? And the clothes... Michael was confounded by the clothes as had been the rest of his investigative squad. They made no sense to him. Michael paced the floor, from his couch to the window and back to the couch again, tossing a small Nerf basketball overhead and catching it again; his socked feet making no noise against the plush carpet.

The autopsy reports on the first two victims didn't glean any additional insight. He knew the cause of death. He knew where the women were found, what they were wearing. He didn't know why they were dead. There were no defensive wounds so whoever killed them overpowered them somehow. Michael needed answers. How could he lead his team without them?

There was a cool dankness in the air. No matter how many times Chloe had done it before, she was always struck with the sterility of death in the morgue. Regardless of how the victims may have died, the morgue was spit shine clean. The stainless steel temporary encasements gleamed with no sign of blood or tell-tale decomposition. The medical examiner, in pristine scrubs nodded his head acknowledging the presence of the onlookers – Dr. Daniels, Addison and Detective Phillips. Addison would just as soon skip this part. She never got used to the idea of being present for autopsy but it came with the job. She readied the tape recorder for the medical examiner's presentation.

The medical examiner, Dr. Wakefield Brookes, pulled back the crisp white sheet and folded it neatly at the pubic hair line of the decedent. The thick layers of makeup had all been removed leaving only the victims real face; ashen and blank. The strangulation marks were more visible today than they were yesterday, standing out as long reddish purple lines against the victims' chocolate skin. There was a small tattoo of a rose with thorns on the decedent's right breast. It had been previously hidden by the clown clothes the perpetrator made her wear. As he continued to process the body, Dr. Brookes made note of evidenced petechial from ruptured blood vessels of the victims' eyes. He noted the ligature marks to the neck as well as some scrapes and abrasions to the knees. As he continued the examination, Dr. Brookes stopped and drew the groups' attention to Jane Doe's left ankle.

"There is some unnatural scarring here." The medical examiner slowly turned Jane Doe's ankle from side to side to get a better look. Phillips and Dr. Daniels took a step forward, closer to the deceased.

"Upon closer examination, there is evidence of a tattoo, I suspect wrapped around the victims ankle. It appears some abrasive solvent was used to erase any identifying markings." The medical examiner reached over to the table and pulled a long cotton swab and proceeded to wipe the area. He encased the swab in a long clear tube and marked it.

"I'll send the sample off to determine what the solvent was. Not sure whether the lab will be able to recreate the tattoo but we will see."

"The perpetrator must not have seen the tattoo on the breast," Dr. Daniels speculated. "Maybe when she disrobed and clothed the vic the tattoo was covered by her bra."

"That would make sense as to why the abrasive agent wasn't used on the upper tattoo," Dr. Brookes supposed.

"I wonder if it will help with identification," Detective Phillips inquired. The medical examiner moved closer to the body and examined the victim's rose markings. Although every tattoo is different, a rose is common. Size and coloring may vary but the tattoo itself was ordinary. The examiner was looking specifically for original markings to differentiate this rose tattoo from all the others he'd seen in his many years of dealing with the deceased.

"There are no special demarcations, no initials to speak of," the examiner advised, lifting up from the body and speaking to the onlookers.

"I've already taken photos. I'll make sure you all get a copy. It still may help with identifying the victim."

The medical examiner made his first cut into Jane Doe, narrating as he went. From the thin razor sharp slice, thick maroon blood revealed itself. He meticulously worked through every organ and over every inch of the victims' body for further clues. As he was wrapping up he offered Detective Phillips and Dr. Daniels a few additional bits of information.

"My unofficial recommended findings are homicide via strangulation. Because of the state of rigor mortis and decomposition, it is my professional opinion that the victim was found within 12 to 16 hours of death. There were no true defensive wounds. I did note some swelling to the back of the head post-mortem. Unsure as to the cause. The abrasions on the victims' knees may have been from falling or dragging during the strangulation itself. Upon examination of the stomach contents, it looks like the decedent hadn't eaten in 24 hours. I will be taking fingerprints and molds of the victims' teeth. Any questions?"

"Doctor, would you say that the findings from this examination are similar to that of the other two women brought in under similar condition?" Dr. Daniels inquired.

"Yes, I would have to say the similarities would suggest these cases are connected. The lack of DNA evidence from the perpetrator, the absence of defensive wounds and of course the makeup and costuming would indeed point to connectivity."

"Any noted differences?" Detective Phillips asked.

"Yes, the scarring to the ankle is new in this case. It wasn't noted in the others, more likely because the other women didn't have any tattoos or other identifying marks."

"Any ideas as to what kind of instrument was used in the strangulation?" Dr. Daniels followed.

"I can't say with any certainty what was used. I can say the same instrument was used with all three victims," the medical examiner offered.

"Any signs of sexual assault?" Dr. Daniels inquired.

"No, there were no signs of sexual assault, not with this victim or the other two," the medical examiner replied. Dr. Daniels found that curious, unsure whether the information or the lack thereof would give insight into the gender of the killer.

Once Dr. Daniels and Detective Phillips finished with their questions, the medical examiner advised that he would send Detective Phillips his full report. Just as they were preparing to leave, Dr. Daniels asked another question.

"Her clothes... what about her clothes?"

"What do you mean?" Dr. Brookes asked. Phillips turned around, interested in the question as well.

"Can you tell anything from the clothes?"

The medical examiner pulled the white sheet up over the body, and rubbed the back of his hand against his forehead.

"There were no foreign hairs on the clothes when we first looked at them. The forensic lab is doing further testing to see what can be extrapolated – whether there are microscopic fibers, possible DNA. We won't know what they determine for at least another 48-to 72 hours if that."

It seemed like another dead end to Phillips, if not completely dead it would be a while before they could learn anything from it.

Addison ended their recording and the three entered the hall.

"I need to get my hands on those clothes," Dr. Daniels mused as the three proceeded down the hall.

"It will be a while like the doc said but I'll see what I can do," Detective Phillips replied.

Chloe had to be satisfied with Phillips response. She knew it was something he had no direct control over.

"Detective Phillips, when I went over the files you sent last night, I noticed that fingerprints for the first two victims had been cross-referenced with missing persons in Georgia. Don't you think expanding the search is warranted at this point?"

"I had that same thought Dr. Daniels. I've already made contact with the necessary parties and our victims' fingerprints are being submitted in the nationwide database."

"That's good to know. Make sure to keep me posted as to the results," Dr. Daniels advised as the group rounded the corner and neared the front door.

"I will." Detective Phillips held the door open as both women exited the medical examiner's office and stepped into the warm spring air. The group began to separate.

"Dr. Daniels, when do you think you'll be ready to present the profile to my detectives?" Chloe knew the question was coming and didn't have an answer. That's the part she hated most. "I wish I could say I was ready now but with so little to go on, I'm not sure that what I could tell you would offer any great insight."

"Understandable. Just let me know when you're ready and I'll make my team available to you."

"Thank you detective."

Chloe knew whether the police came up with anything else immediately or not, she had to come up with a profile. At this point nothing was really clear. She would have to go back to the beginning and scour whatever information she had. Chloe was still bothered; bothered by the fact the fingerprints from the victims had not been run outside of Georgia. One unknown body was cause, two unknown murder victims was beyond cause to extend the search. With three bodies the police were just now taking proactive steps to try and figure out who these girls were? Yeah, Chloe was having a major problem with that one. Part of her suspected why more aggressive investigative techniques had not been instituted in this situation. She would try to reserve judgment but it would be difficult. Even though it was still early morning, Dr. Daniels knew she was in for another long day.

Anna tagged along for the remainder of Nurse Drysdale's rounds. She was looking for her perfect next needy soul. At the moment, Mr. Dunn remained at the top of the list. Anna chose him because he was kind of obnoxious more than anything. Anna was hankering for another assist. It had been a while since she helped a patient out of their misery.

The final stop of rounds was the wing where the terminally ill patients were. Anna had to refrain from rubbing her hands together like a fat man ready for a good meal. There was an extra bit of pep in her step as she followed in Nurse Sophie Lynn's footsteps, eager to see who was in each room.

But first they had to make a pit stop at the little pharmacy closet.

"How's it going Sophie Lynn," a spry older woman from behind the counter asked. Her purply gray hair was reminiscent of the 50's in a high beehive, and her steel-rimmed glasses perched on the edge of her nose, held in place by a long sparkly eyeglass chain.

"Hey there Sylvia, you doing alright today?"

"The good Lord allowed these eyes of mine to open and these feet of mine to move. I would say I am having a great day," she replied happily. "Who's the new girl," Ms. Sylvia asked as if Anna wasn't standing there.

"This is Anna Montgomery. She's gonna be helping on second shift."

"Well there Anna, welcome to the Archibald family. Glad to have ya."

Anna nodded in receipt of the overly warm welcome. She was much more interested in what was behind the attendant than engaging in conversation with her. There were rows upon rows of bottled medication. Anna took note of the shelf with the syringes as well as the small locked wall cabinet immediately behind Sylvia's head.

"I need to pick up a few things before we make the last round," Nurse Drysdale said, reeling Anna back into the conversation.

"Well I'm ready when you are," Sylvia shot back.

"I need 800 cc's butabarbital for room 214. I also need 15 cc's of insulin for room 278. I need tramadol, two tablets 600 milligrams for room 255 and injectable 1200 cc's for 256."

"Give me just a sec," Sylvia replied, slowly getting up from her stool. Her affect was spry but her body defied her perky attitude.

Sylvia methodically made her way to retrieve the items Nurse Drysdale requested. Anna watched her intently; seeing what medicines were readily available on the shelves and those that needed to be retrieved from the locked cabinet. The tramadol; a highly potent sedative was locked away, as was the butabarbital. The insulin Sylvia retrieved from a shelf. Duly noted. Anna refocused her attention so as to not look suspicious.

Finally, Sylvia returned with the medications. Nurse Drysdale had to sign for each one. There was no new-fangled electronic tracking system but rather old fashioned pen and paper verification. That worked for Anna. She smiled widely at Sylvia before leaving. Anna knew she would have to make nice with the old lady to get access to what she would need.

"It was so good to meet you Ms. Sylvia. I am sure I will be seeing you around." Anna poured on the charm and even took on a bit of the southern drawl to sell herself as one of them. Ms. Sylvia soaked it right up.

"Oh we'll definitely see each other again. Ya'll take care now, ya hear?"

Nurse Drysdale and Anna moved to the last hall of patients. Anna noticed that quite a few of the rooms were vacant. It was kind of a letdown. She'd hope there would be a plethora of deathly ill patients to choose from but things didn't seem to be working out that way.

"There's a lot of empty rooms," Anna observed in an effort to get an explanation from Sophie Lynn.

"Rarely is this wing full. The worst of them are transferred to hospice because there was nothing more the hospital could do. Of course, with their conditions, some of the patients pass on. It's just the hard truth. Terminal patients die... sad though..." Nurse Drysdale continued. "No matter how long I've been nursing, it always hurts when one of my patients doesn't make it."

Anna listened. Nurse Sophie Lynn seemed to have a heart after all. Maybe she misjudged her in the beginning.

"I think when they leave this world, they go to a better place. No more pain, no more suffering... so I'm never sad for them."

There was a brief pause in Sophie Lynn's step as she listened to what her new charge had to say.

"I guess there's some merit to that argument as well. Hadn't really thought about it that way," she said reflectively.

Anna was pleased with herself; reaffirming why she did the things she did. As the two entered the first room with a patient in it, Anna perked up.

The atmosphere in the room was much more somber. There was no bright greeting from Nurse Drysdale. Rather, she entered quietly. The only sound that could be heard was labored breathing and the constant tic of the machines surrounding the patient.

Sophie Lynn lifted the chart from the end of the bed and scanned the notes the attending physician left. She then approached the side of the bed very quietly, as though she were tiptoeing. Anna followed suit peering over the nurses' shoulder to get a good look at the patient.

"Hey there Ms. Jane."

There was no verbal response from the patient. She wasn't able to speak with the breathing tube down her throat. Instead Ms. Jane responded with her eyes. She looked in Ms. Jane's direction and blinked. It was probably the best she could do.

"Ms. Jane has brain cancer. The tumor has metastasized so she doesn't have much longer. We just try to keep her pain manageable."

Nurse Drysdale began the administration of the liquid tramadol straight into the intravenous line that fed into the patient's bony wrist.

The saddest part is, nobody comes to visit her. She'll probably die alone with nobody to stand at her graveside."

Sad for Ms. Jane, but in Anna's calculative mind, no family was a bonus. Nurse Drysdale emptied the full syringe into the IV tube; making sure to depress the medication slowly to avoid bubbles in the line. Air bubbles in the intravenous line could travel to the patient's vital organs and cause significant complications and Nurse Drysdale didn't want to make the matter any worse for her patient. Ms. Jane looked as if the pain medicine started to work instantly as her eyes began to slowly close and the heart monitor regulated at a slower rate. Maybe it was just wishful thinking on the part of the nurses but Ms. Jane's breathing seemed to level out as well. As Nurse Drysdale and Nurse Montgomery left the room, Anna moved the lovely Ms. Jane to the top of her list for assistance.

Anna moved with anticipation to the next occupied room. The patient, although really sick, didn't strike Anna in the same way as Mr. Dunn or Ms. Jane. They would not make the list. The last occupied room closest to the nurses' station on the terminal wing was room 214. Once again, Nurse Drysdale was relatively quiet as she processed into the single occupancy room. Anna was surprised when she looked at the patient. She expected an elderly person. Instead, she saw a young lady, maybe a few years her junior. The one thing that was similar to the other terminal patients on the wing was the amount of machinery hooked up, virtually keeping the patient alive.

"Abigail was in a horrible car accident about a month ago. Damn near wrapped her car around a pole, driving too fast and drinking too much. Broke nearly every bone in her body. Did a lot of internal damage. Came down from Grady Hospital maybe a week or so ago. She's in a medically induced coma. The healing process is very painful." Nurse Drysdale continued to perform her duties as Anna looked on.

"She was the lucky one," Nurse Sophie Lynn said, as she tucked in the edge of Abigail's crisp white sheets.

"What do you mean lucky," Anna inquired.

Sophie Lynn paused for a moment and then responded. "She hit another vehicle before the car came to rest at the pole. The mother and little boy in the other car died instantly."

"Oh no," Anna replied. "That's terrible."

"Sure is," Sophie Lynn continued. "Nearly split the town in two; some folks calling for Abigail to be prosecuted, other folks feeling sorry for her because she was troubled. Been troubled a long time with that good for nothin' momma of hers."

Anna waited, eager for Sophie Lynn to delve deeper into the story. They didn't have to be mindful of Abigail hearing them or feel bad about talking about her in front of her face. She couldn't hear them anyway. Anna was intrigued. She found it very difficult to hide her excitement so she busied herself with the doctor's chart so Sophie Lynn wouldn't see the devilish grin that crept over her face. There was no need to greet Abigail or make nice with her. Nurse Drysdale administered the barbiturate from two syringes and checked the patient's vitals. She shared them aloud with Anna who dutifully recorded them on the chart.

Sophie Lynn sighed deeply as she finished up in the patient's room. The two nurses walked out into the hallway, allowing the patient's door to close on its own.

"Now, I'm not one for gossiping," Sophie Lynn advised, "but telling the truth about a thing ain't what I call gossip."

Anna leaned one the counter after they arrived back at the nurses' station as Sophie Lynn continued.

"It's really a tragedy all the way around," Sophie Lynn said. Even though the hallway was nearly abandoned, she dropped her voice so no one but Anna could hear. "Abigail's momma has been a drunk dope fiend and a loose woman since she dropped out of high school. Men in and out of the house… she didn't protect her daughter from what was going on and poor Abigail followed right down that same tragic path... I mean what choices did she really have? You do what you know..."

Anna saw sympathy in Nurse Drysdale's eyes and heard empathy in her voice.

"That's how it is in a small town Anna Montgomery. Everybody knows your business. I'm sure you're not used to that but if you aim to stay here, everybody will know exactly who Anna Montgomery is."

Whether it was a word of caution or not, Anna took it in stride. Sophie Lynn's comments certainly reminded her that she didn't have a lot of time to leave her mark in Thomasville.

That evening, as Anna prepared for bed back at the boarding house, she considered her prospects. Just thinking about their dire circumstances and how much she could help them made Anna feel giddy like a school girl. Mr. Dunn quickly lost ranking. He was ornery but nothing terribly special. Anna would just as soon leave him be unless she had time. Anna understood that she was definitely pressed for time; not like before when she had the opportunity to injure and rescue and feed her heroic tendencies. There were people looking for Anna, accusing her of all manner of evil. They misunderstood her calling, the good she did for the world. So Anna didn't have a whole lot of time to make the kind of impact she desired at Archibald. She had to be swift and smart and help as many patients as she could before it was time to move on.

The top two contenders were Ms. Jane and of course Abigail. As Anna lay in bed looking up at the ceiling, she contemplated who would be first. Ms. Jane... sweet old lady Jane. She deserved mercy. Her days of suffering had been long and Anna desired to help her transition. It would almost be like a mercy killing. With no family to speak of, there wouldn't be too much fuss or attention after Anna helped her cross over. That was definitely a bonus for Ms. Jane. But dear sweet drunken Abigail... Anna smiled widely as she contemplated the young ladies' plight. Abigail was both a victim and a murderer herself. According to Sophie Lynn, sentiments in the town ran high about this girl so anything that happened to her would certainly add gasoline to a fire that was already burning. It was a high profile case and the attention would be incredible if Abigail met an untimely end.

As Anna closed her eyes and prepared for a night's rest, she made her decision. Both of her potential victims had been long suffering, each in her own way. They both needed the kind of help only Anna could offer. She was happy for them. Soon it would be over and they wouldn't have to deal with any more tragedies in their own pitiful little lives. Jane would be first. Freeing Ms. Jane from her suffering would make good practice to see what Archibald hospital's response time was like. Mercifully killing old Ms. Jane would be a perfect precursor to what Anna knew would be an epic kill.

Anna started to rock herself to sleep. The lyrics of her favorite lullaby popped in her head and she started to hum the familiar chorus...

"Hush little baby don't say a word..."

Chapter Four

She was up before the sun. Grace Pembroke Wetherby experienced a cadre of emotions anticipating the arrival of the new house girl. Embittered by her husband's previous deception and emblazoned by her father's words of wisdom, Grace couldn't resist fantasizing about what she knew was to come. She'd gotten better. The first one was really a test, proving ground to see if she really had the stomach for it. She managed to pull it off. It wasn't smooth and she paid for it afterward by spilling her stomach's contents on her fancy floors and wallowing in nightmares from the girls' choked screams. But anger was a powerful motivator and even though her husband's infidelity happened a little over a year ago, Grace still wore the wounds like battle scars. She was now waging war; war on any good for nothing, low life black bitch that reminded her of the ultimate betrayal.

Grace never looked at her husband Drake the same way. Of course, he apologized profusely and promised he'd never do such a thing again. She desperately wanted to believe him. Had he cheated on her with a woman worthy of him, it would have been one thing. But he decided to fuck the spook hired to cook, clean and babysit. That's what made his deception so horribly painful. Grace told him she forgave him and she did, to a point. He was just a man, tempted by lascivious, wanton nigger flesh flashed in his unassuming face. Adding insult to injury, her children, Mary Lou and Preston, loved the slut that cared for them. When Grace fired the sleazy bitch, her children pouted and cried for days. Grace was incensed.

As Grace prepared for her day, she thought fondly of her father. He was a great man who lived on biblical principles and the tenets this country was founded on. Old man Pembroke didn't believe in race mixing. It was a fact niggers were inferior; history proved that and contemporary times were a testament to how unintelligent, shiesty and worthless Black folks really were. Grace wasn't a racist. She merely understood that Whites were superior. People could argue from emotion but they couldn't argue with the facts. The superiority of the White race was a fact, plain and simple.

Soon it would be time to get her children up for school and kiss her husband goodbye before he left for work. Yeah, she still fulfilled some parts of her wifely responsibility. Regardless of how much she hated Drake at times, she didn't want to lose him. He was her children's father and his finances made it possible for her to live the life she had grown accustomed to. Grace wouldn't sacrifice that and settle for less because of his ill-timed slip up. That would mean the coon won. That was an impossibility in Grace's world.

Grace made her way to the kitchen and put on a pot of coffee. It was in the quiet times, much like this morning that she thought about everything that'd transpired over the past few months. Sitting at the marble island, her coffee steaming in its porcelain cup, Grace smiled, reliving those virgin moments. She had a knack for it, killing that is. Grace knew going in what her intentions were in hiring that first girl. She couldn't get the original whore that slept with her husband but she could still exact revenge. That first girl... Grace didn't care to remember her name, the details of who she was were unimportant. As a matter of fact, it wasn't important that her features were like that of the harlot who slept with her husband. All black folks looked the same. And the first girl she killed was perfect. Grace ran an ad for a nanny/housekeeper. There were many who responded to the ad of all races, ages and levels of experience. Grace's criteria was simple... young, small in stature so she would be easy to overpower and a nigger. When she saw the girl, Grace knew immediately she was the one. Grace hired her on the spot and the girl reported to work the next morning.

It was all about the planning for Grace. She'd been planning for months. Grace cried a few nights after her husband spoiled himself with the help, but not long after Grace's crying spells dried up and a plan started to formulate in her mind. She would make them pay and pay with their lives.

Besides, who would miss a few low-life scoundrel jungle bunnies anyway? Killing off a few would make her feel a whole lot better about the situation.

That night, after hiring the first girl, Grace was excited; nervous, but excited. As she sat at her Singer sewing machine; her pale hands covered with milky white latex gloves as she crafted the jigaboo's outfit, Grace contemplated the easiest and most efficient ways to get rid of her. Nothing messy, Grace wasn't in to getting her hands dirty and wanted no evidence left to have to contend with. Quick, easy and clean was the way to go. Grace tossed and turned that night. Could she really do it? Would the girl fight back causing a major altercation? Would she get caught? The questions rolled around in her head as she contemplated pulling off the ultimate revenge.

The next morning, just like this morning, Grace felt ready. She was committed to the process and once the girl showed up, it was too late for second guessing. The girl was all smiles. She was happy to be there. Grace showed her around just enough to keep up the façade; going over her responsibilities and even introducing her to the family. She wanted to see what their reaction was to the new girl; whether her children would instantly warm up to her as they had done with the first one and especially how her husband would respond. When he smiled and politely shook the girls hand, maintaining eye contact longer than Grace would have liked, Grace was convinced more than ever that what she intended to do was the right thing. Drake was weak, still weak for scrapings from the bottom of the human barrel.

Once her family was safely out of the home and moving on with their day, it was time for Grace to handle the matter at hand. The laundry room proved to be the perfect place. It was close to the garage and far enough from the rest of the house that if there was a problem it could be easily remedied. None of her expensive home furnishings were at risk of being damaged in the laundry area. That certainly wouldn't do. She lured the girl in under the guise of explaining how she preferred the family's laundry to be handled. When the bitch bent down to look inside the front loading washer, Grace struck.

Squeezing the life out of the spook was exhilarating. Grace's heart was pumping so loudly she could hear each beat thundering in her ears. The girl wanted to fight, she tried to fight but Grace would not be denied. Grace could still hear the curdled screams choked short in the girls' throat. She kicked and flailed her arms but Grace planted her feet firmly and lifted into the chokehold refusing to let go. And then there was silence and the bitch fell limp. Grace let her fall to the floor. Realizing the girl was dead, Grace was giddy with excitement. Adrenaline coursed freely through her veins and she was ecstatic.

It was cumbersome stripping the girl and changing her clothes into the outfit Grace sewed by hand for her. The cheap dollar store makeup she bought, just for the occasion, put the finishing touches on the mockery of a woman laid before her. It was therapeutic painting the ugly face, showing what she truly represented to the world... a clown... a shuckin', jiving and husband fuckin clown...That same high is what Grace expected for the day.

It was 5:15 in the morning. The angst Grace felt intensified. After the first one, the following day, Drake asked about the newly hired help. Initially, Grace was panic stricken not knowing what to say. She longed to tell him exactly what happened; that because of how he'd hurt her she resorted to murder. But Drake would never understand that. He thought he'd been forgiven and the whole affair was a thing of the past. He had no idea Grace had been affected so pervasively.

She wondered if he would have questions about the new girl, this Tanquilla girl. Of course, she would make sure he saw her, gauge his reaction, see if his eyes lit up and then dropped for fear Grace would notice. Having a new girl was a reminder of what he'd done with the last and Grace needed him to have that reminder. It was her passive aggressive way of getting at him. For her not to have help in the house would be odd. They'd always had a girl. It would be too easy to keep the girl away from him. Where was the fun in that?

Chief Livingston dreaded the start of his day. After meeting with the Chief of Communications for the police department and his immediate supervisor, getting his ass handed to him on a silver platter, Livingston prepared to meet with the press. Bloodsucking vultures, he thought to himself as he straightened his tie. The media mob had already gathered in front of the building. There were a lot of facets to his job that he despised. The mandatory brown nosing and never-ending bureaucratic red tape were near the top of the list, with the malicious media at the pinnacle.

"Chief, they're ready for you," Detective Phillips advised knocking on the door and swinging it open simultaneously.

"Let's get this shit over with. Is Daniels here?" The Chief's disgruntled response wasn't new to Detective Phillips. He was no fan of the media either.

"Yes sir. I understand she is in the lobby."

Chief Livingston moved towards the door. Phillips stepped aside and fell in step with him towards the elevators. The two men rode down in silence. Livingston's agitation was evident as he shifted his weight from one foot to the other and mumbled things Phillips didn't quite understand. When the elevator doors opened, Livingston walked out with authority. He nodded to Dr. Daniels and the trio moved forward in unison to the front door.

Before the door opened the buzz amongst the crowd rose to a fevered pitch. Bright lights flashed from multiple directions. Reporters attempted to ask questions even before a statement was made. Chief Livingston stepped to the podium. Dr. Daniels and Detective Phillips stood slightly behind him. With the plethora of microphones attached, the slightest sound could be heard. Livingston cleared his throat. The audience of media persons and a large crowd of onlookers fell silent.

"Good morning. I'm going to make this quick. There have been three murders linked together based on crime scene evidence. All three victims have been found along major interstates under overpasses. We are asking-"

"Isn't it true there is a serial killer on the loose?" A reporter shouted from the crowd.

"Any comment about the baby doll killer, Chief?" Another yelled out.

Chief Livingston's agitation grew but he tried to keep a cool head.

"We are asking the citizens of Atlanta to be especially vigilant and careful," he replied ignoring the obvious. "Thank you."

As the Chief turned his back on the crowd he was plundered with question after question that he summarily dismissed. Dr. Daniels and Detective Phillips followed him back in. Once the three were in the elevator and the door securely closed in front of them, Chief Livingston spoke.

"Whatever you have to do to close this case, do it! We are going to have all out panic in the streets with this serial killer thing, so handle it!"

Chief Livingston stormed out of the elevator leaving Chloe and Michael in his wake. The look between the two of them spoke volumes without a word being uttered. As the elevator travelled down, Michael tried to maintain his focus on the business at hand. Being alone with Chloe was always difficult. He had to suppress his masculinized tendencies but he found it increasingly problematic. Michael was completely intrigued by her. She would know it soon but now was not the time. When the elevator arrived on his floor he offered parting salutations and stepped off. Chloe returned his greeting in kind. Their eyes met as the door closed.

Back in the lobby, Addison fell in line with Dr. Daniels.

"Is the car out front?"

"No, I parked it in the back to avoid the press," Addison replied.

"Excellent," Chloe said.

It was 6:00 a.m. Grace climbed the stairs, and upon entering each of her children's bedrooms, turned on the light and encouraged Mary Lou and Preston to get up. As expected, Mary Lou jumped right up in response to her mom's call. Preston on the other hand was a little harder to get moving.

"Come on Preston, time for school," Grace insisted, crossing the room and pulling the covers back on her son.

"I can't go to school, I don't feel well," Preston replied, reaching for and pulling the covers up over his head. Grace didn't have time for his antics. Not long on patience, Grace sat on the end of her son's bed and pulled the covers down again.

"Preston, let me feel your head." Preston lifted himself up and Grace reluctantly placed the back of her hand to his head.

"You don't have a fever."

"But my stomach hurts," Preston whined.

"I don't have time for this. Get up, get cleaned up, you are going to school." Grace left the room without looking back. It was 6:15.

Preston grumbled. He knew that tone and decided not to push it any further. He really didn't feel well but his mother had spoken.

Grace made her way to the kitchen to prepare her children's breakfast. She did so every morning. It was a part of their routine. It was important to maintain the routine. Grace relished in the knowledge that soon she would be able to command life and death. There was power in that feeling; power that was zapped from her when her husband defiled their marital bed. She smiled as she scrambled the eggs and attended to the toaster. Not long after, she heard the familiar footsteps of her children. They were honoring the schedule. Mary Lou sat down, said grace and immediately began to eat when her mother placed the plate before her. Preston didn't move as readily. He said his prayer as he'd been taught, but pushed the food around the plate as though it was unappealing.

The doorbell rang. Grace looked at the kitchen clock. The girl was right on time. If this were to be a long term assignment Grace might have been impressed with her punctuality. But she would only be here for a short while.

"Who's at the door mommy?" Mary Lou asked, her curiosity getting the better of her.

"The help," Grace responded flatly. She moved towards the front door. Through the three inch glass she could see the goofy smile on the girls' face. Grace plastered on a fictitious smile of her own, willing to create the façade of this being a pleasant experience.

"Good morning Mrs. Wetherby," Tangela beamed as soon as the door was opened. Grace heard the heaviness of her husband's footsteps descending the staircase.

"Good morning... Tan..."

"Tangela," she continued to smile.

"That's right, Tangela." Grace stepped aside and allowed the girl to enter.

"How'd you get here this morning?" Grace peeped outside the door and saw a car she hadn't seen the first time.

"Oh, I drove," Tangela replied crossing the threshold.

Dammit. This was a contingency Grace hadn't planned for. She'd been so careful with the others. She'd asked them about transportation and if they had a car. Grace insisted they use public transportation to get to her home. She'd even sprung for a cab on a couple of occasions but failed to do so with this one. She would have to take added measures to clean up behind herself. That did not please Grace. Closing the door, Grace instructed the girl to follow her.

"Make sure to wipe your feet at the door," she chided.

Tangela took special care to do as she was asked. Although she thought it odd since it was a bright sunny day, Tangela didn't want to question her new employer's quirks. Entering the kitchen, Mary Lou was the first to speak.

"Mom, is this our new nanny?" Mary Lou said brightly.

Grace introduced the girl to her children. "Yes Mary Lou, Preston, this is Tangelia. We're going to try her out and see if she fits with our family."

"Good morning Mary Lou and Preston, so nice to meet you both."

Mary Lou greeted Tangela with a warm smile. Preston waved; his stomach revolting.

"Preston, eat your breakfast, you need your strength for the day," Grace encouraged.

Preston grimaced. "Yes ma'am." He put a fork full of eggs in his mouth and chewed slowly, grimacing as the yellowed concoction hit his troubled stomach. Mr. Wetherby entered the kitchen. Grace made a special point to watch him as he saw the new help.

"Good morning," Mr. Wetherby said cheerily; far too cheerily to Grace's liking. She saw him smiling like a horny Cheshire cat at the girl. Grace was immediately incensed but kept her expression cool.

"Good morning sir," the girl replied. She didn't allow her gaze to linger even though Mr. Wetherby seemed to be having a much more difficult time disengaging his eyes from her.

"Is there anything I can help with this morning?" Tangela inquired.

"Yes, clean up the mornings dishes. Once the children are off to school, we'll discuss what else needs to be done."

"I'm finished Ms. Tangela," Mary Lou squealed. Grace liked the fact that her daughter was so respectful, just not to the help. The jigaboo didn't deserve such respect. She was nothing... a nobody."

"Excellent Ms. Mary Lou, I'll take that plate from you." Tangela and the young girl exchanged smiles. Grace's stomach turned violently. She couldn't wait to be done with her newest catch.

"Preston, what about you?" Tangela asked.

"Mmhmmm," Preston murmured. His skin was moist and lacked color. Mr. Wetherby drank his coffee at the counter. Grace noted that his eyes continued to travel in the direction of the girl. Grace was repulsed. He was such a pig.

"Aren't you going to be late dear?" There was a bite to her question her husband understood. He quickly straightened himself up, averting any further eye contact with the new nanny and finished his last gulp of coffee.

"You're right dear," he said, leaning over and kissing Grace on the cheek she extended to him. She rarely allowed him to kiss her on the lips anymore. She knew where those things had been.

"See you later kids," Mr. Wetherby said, grabbing his briefcase from near the entrance to the kitchen.

"Bye dad," Mary Lou replied cheerfully. Preston managed a wave. Mr. Wetherby couldn't resist nodding to the new girl as he hastily made his way to the garage entrance.

"Get your backpacks. The bus should be here shortly," Grace encouraged, doing all she could to keep things on schedule. Tangela turned toward the sink to handle the first mornings work.

Chairs scooted back, Mary Lou and Preston responded to their mother's instruction. There was a splat and a malodorous stench wafted in the air.

"Dammit Preston!" Grace yelled. She rarely used profanity around her children but this time it was warranted. Her son's stomach upset emptied onto her kitchen floor. Preston stood doubled over, dry heaving; his face flushed a bilious pink. Then the stench hanging stagnantly in the air elevated. Preston was too sick to be embarrassed.

"You have got to be kidding me," Grace grumbled. Doubling back and walking up behind her son she grabbed him by the belt. "You shit your pants?" She screamed, releasing his pants and pushing Preston forward. He almost fell in his own waste. Mary Lou giggled. Her mother shot her a look that silenced the child instantly. Tears brimmed on Preston's lids, his ill feelings exacerbated by the unfortunate accident and his mothers' disgust.

"Go to the laundry room right now before I do something I'll regret." Preston, head hung in shame, righted himself and slowly moved toward the laundry just off the kitchen. Grace infuriated by his slow pace added insult to injury.

"Move your ass!"

Preston shuffled his feet a little faster. The tears, previously teetering on his lids fell, staining his young cheeks. Mary Lou stifled another giggle, not wanting to turn her mother's wrath her way. She scurried toward the front door to catch the bus. Tangela sprang into action, finding the necessary tools to attend to the mess in the kitchen. Grace turned her attention to Mary Lou, seeing her off. Assured her daughter was safely on the bus, Grace marched back into the house to deal with her son. Breathing heavy, Grace leveled a heated gaze at Tangela, but she was not the target, not yet anyway. Tangela continued to work on the floor, cleaning up Preston's leavings. Crossing the room and entering the laundry area, Grace was livid. This was not a part of the routine and her son's little antics were toying with her schedule.

"What are you just standing there looking stupid for, get those nasty clothes off."

"I told you I was sick, momma," Preston replied helpless and humiliated.

"Don't you dare talk back to me."

Grace moved towards her son, assisting him in taking his clothes off. She yanked so hard it was difficult for Preston to keep his footing. Once she was satisfied that everything had been removed, Grace grabbed a folded towel from off the table and shoved it towards Preston.

"Cover up, get in the tub and clean yourself off, and go straight to bed." Preston didn't respond. Had his mother listened to him in the beginning the whole situation could have been avoided. Still feeling queasy, Preston did as he was told, taking the back staircase up to the bathroom. His mother wouldn't have to say anything else to him. He would do as she told him so he could get back in the bed.

Grace violently threw the clothes in the front loading washing machine. Slamming the door and starting the machine, she left the laundry and abruptly rounded the corner into the kitchen.

"Are you finished yet?" She whirled on Tangela expecting the lazy coon to be goofing off. Instead she found Tangela had attended to the mess and was finishing up with the dishes. It didn't stop her from ranting.

"When you finish, come into the living room. You've got work to do."

Grace didn't wait for a response and left the room. She flounced on the couch, disconcerted with the events of the morning. Grace knew she had to gain her composure or the rest of her day would be equally as disruptive. Closing her eyes for a moment, Grace concentrated on leveling her breathing. She couldn't afford to scare off the help. She needed this kill to make herself feel better.

Chapter Five

Anna was excited for the day. She could hardly sleep after her first full shift at Archibald Hospital. Although housekeeping services were provided in Mrs. Jenkins boarding house, Anna took the time to spread up her bed before dressing for work. The early morning news was on the television. Anna was deep in her own blissful thoughts about the prospects for the day as the television droned on in the background. Anna took a hot shower and afterward stood in the bathroom with a towel wrapped about her thin frame, brushing her teeth. She meandered back into the bedroom portion of her accommodations as she continued to brush.

"Chief Blake Livingston was bombarded with questions after making the announcement that a series of murders in and around metropolitan Atlanta are indeed the work of a serial killer. The baby doll killer, as some are calling the assailant, has left the Atlanta Police Department scrambling to figure out who the killer is and exactly who the victims are. This on the heels of the notorious Death Angel Killer, Anna Black, who is still on the loose, has the city of Atlanta reeling. Reporting live, Johnathan Fredericks, News Center One."

The toothbrush nearly fell from Anna's mouth as she watched the replay of the news from the day before. She felt two things; exhilaration and aggravation, the duality of which perplexed and infuriated Anna. She still managed to evade capture which gave Anna a chance to help more people. That was the exhilarating part. But now, someone else was stealing the spotlight; diverting her well-earned and much deserved attention for her incredible acts of bravery. That was the aggravating part. Anna didn't appreciate being an afterthought; running as an "oh by the way" to someone else's debauchery. Anna would have to change the narrative, and quick.

Anna could hardly wait to report into work. It was difficult occupying herself until the afternoon shift began. Anna decided to explore the fair town of Thomasville to kill some time.

"Good morning Ms. Montgomery." Anna was greeted by Ms. Jenkins, the owner of the boarding house.

"Morning."

"Did you sleep well dear," Ms. Jenkins asked as she shuffled papers at the makeshift front desk. Anna's attention was temporarily distracted as she noted the television on the desk behind Ms. Jenkins, tuned into the same news station she had been watching.

"Dear, are you okay? All the color has drained from your face?"

"Oh no, I'm fine," Anna replied, forcing herself to refocus on Ms. Jenkins. "I didn't eat dinner after I got off work last night and now I'm starving!" Anna rubbed her cheeks with both hands encouraging some color to return.

"That I do understand. Honey, with this sugar condition, I have to make sure I eat on a regular basis. Can't afford to let my numbers get out of whack," Ms. Jenkins offered. Anna took another look at Ms. Jenkins. From the girth around her waist, Anna didn't think Ms. Jenkins forgot too many meals.

"You should go up the block to Andy's," Ms. Jenkins suggested. "They have a great menu, plenty of good southern comfort to choose from." There was a glint in Ms. Jenkins eyes as she talked about a place anyone could tell she frequented.

"I just might do that," Anna replied. "Thank you Ms. Jenkins. See you later."

"Have a good day dear," Ms. Jenkins replied, turning her attention back to the television set. "Have a good ..."

Anna was out of the door and headed to Andy's before Ms. Jenkins mouth fell open at the sight of someone familiar on her television. She couldn't believe what she was seeing. Turning up the volume, Ms. Jenkins paid close attention to what the reporter was saying.

She'd nervously watched the news, waiting to hear those fateful words that would make her latest pastime more costly than she would allow herself to recognize. Grace hung on every word the chief of police said and didn't say. They knew some things but not enough. She still had a secret; one that made her smile uncontrollably and nothing the cop said gave her pause. Her mission was clear. There were wrongs that still needed to be righted and Grace was convinced more than ever that she was doing the right thing. Her father would be so proud of her. Knowing that made Grace's heart swell.

Hush

Grace sat in front of her Singer sewing machine crafting the next outfit. This was her time. The children were resting comfortably and Drake was in the library enjoying a late night drink that would soon have him resting in a self-induced coma-like state. His drinking increased after she deprived him of what he desired most. Whether that was her or the black harlot he slept with, Grace wasn't sure. Either way, Drake would be out of her hair soon enough. Toast to you, you slimy bastard, Grace thought as the Singer buzzed in the background. She needed for that to happen sooner rather than later; for Drake to fall drunkenly into the bed and fall asleep. He wouldn't interrupt her in the sewing room. He understood that to be her space. Just like too many nights before, they would go to bed separately. Sex between the two had been strained for a while and Drake had grown tired of begging his wife to fulfill his manly needs. He knew better than to bother her with that. When she was ready, if she was ready, she would be with him in that way. But she wasn't ready yet. Picturing him with that nigger troll, using his manhood in such a depraved way, repulsed Grace. No, she wasn't ready to share what was hers again. That was part of Drake's punishment for being so damn gullible; unable to resist the temptation of black trash.

Killing Tangela calmed her in a way that nothing else could. It was her new high, her new orgasm. The power and control she felt in strangling the life out of that last worthless bitch was everything. Grace felt a greater level of achievement with this one. There were some unexpected obstacles she had to contend with that had it been earlier in her murderous spree may have thrown her for a loop. But Grace gained strength and increased knowledge with each kill.

After her daughter was off to school and Preston was tucked away in his room, Grace gave the girl her list of responsibilities for the day. She'd thought long and hard on how to get rid of the damn car, kicking herself for not remembering to tell the stupid bitch not to drive. It was funny to Grace that none of the other girls asked why they shouldn't drive their cars to her home. They were so grateful to have the fucking job they dared not question what their new employer said. They couldn't afford to risk pissing the boss off and potentially losing the job before it was completely secured. But she'd slipped with this last one, anxious to have someone. Tangela was so right for execution, Grace temporarily lost focus. It wouldn't happen again.

She kept Tangela busy attending to Preston during the day. When Mary Lou came home, Grace made sure Tangela attended to both of them. In between, the girl was responsible for housekeeping, even though the house stayed pretty much in pristine condition. Grace found things for her to do; cleaning the crevices of each bathroom's high-end tile with a toothbrush, washing windows, taking out the trash – fitting of course considering the girls' station in life. After dinner, she was responsible for getting the children's homework and getting them prepared for bed. The appointed hour drew nigh. Drake wasn't expected home until well after nine. He found new reasons to stay later at the office every day and Grace never bothered him as to why. She used her time wisely. Grace checked the back corner of her sewing room. She only had a few pair of the black patent leather shoes left. Grace made a note to order more.

The last thing the girl was responsible for doing was to attend to the day's laundry. Grace had the room all prepared; rubber gloves discriminately placed on the shelf, a trusty pair of nylons tucked fingertips away for just the right moment, the girl's new outfit, frilly lace socks and shiny shoes, and of course the makeup Grace would use to make her 'beautiful'. The girl kept good spirits throughout the day no matter what chore or responsibility Grace threw her way. She was a groveling bitch and Grace couldn't wait to be rid of her. In her mind she was on to the next one, calculating how much sooner she would advertise for help.

Grace lured the girl into the laundry room with the promise of her last assignment for the day. She willingly followed, so anxious to please her new boss, still smiling, still so fucking gullible.

"I need for you to take care of the last of the laundry before you leave for the evening."

"No problem Mrs. Wetherby."

Tangela was tired. It had been a good day but she couldn't wait to get home to rest her aching feet. Daycare and working with babies was nothing like what she'd done today, but Mary Lou and Preston even sick, made the experience all worth it.

Tangela bent down to the laundry sorter to retrieve the load of clothes. Finishing up was the only thing on her mind. Suddenly she struggled to breath. She fought against the constriction on her throat. It tightened. She tried to scream. The desperate sound got caught in her throat. Things started to get dark and she fought for the light. Where was the light? Something deep within her wouldn't give in to the darkness trying to encompass her. Tangela struggled to reach the thing that tried to take her out but couldn't. She tried to wedge her fingers between the tightening noose and the flesh of her neck, becoming rawer with each passing moment. The groans and growls she heard in the distance didn't come from her. They came from the one trying to snuff her out.

The light faded. Tangela felt her body failing to fight back. And then, all went dark...

When she slid on the rubberized gloves and took the nylons to the girls' neck, Grace experienced such an adrenaline rush. That feeling didn't fade as she laced the nylon around her hands and pulled... and pulled... and pulled some more. The black bitch tried to fight her, wriggling and grabbing, but all she grabbed was pure air. Grace felt empowered; strengthened by her natural hatred for niggers in general and specific anger for the slut who seduced her husband. This girl became that girl and the feelings of hurt and pain and power oozed from every pore of Grace's being. Gutturally triumphant sounds poured from Grace's thin lips as she won the battle, squeezing every ounce of pitiful life out of her. The girl didn't go down easy but she did go down.

Convinced that her initial work was done, Grace prepared to dispose of the garbage. There was a sound she didn't expect... footsteps moving in her direction. They weren't heavy enough to be Drake's. He wasn't supposed to be home yet.

Peeking out of the laundry room door, Grace determined the source of the noise.

"Mary Lou, what are you doing out of bed?"

Grace attempted to quiet her labored breathing; beads of perspiration dotted her forehead. She wiped at them with the back of her hand. There her daughter stood in a soft yellow night gown with bright pink flowers, holding her sleeping doll. Grace made sure that every doll in Mary Lou's collection looked like her and not like the help.

"I got thirsty mommy."

Mary Lou took a few steps closer to her mother and Grace moved towards her, abbreviating her daughter's forward motion.

"Let me help you so you can get back in bed," Grace offered, placing her hand on her daughter's back and guiding her away from the scene of the crime and towards the refrigerator. She poured her daughter a half a glass of milk and handed it to her, tapping her foot wishing for Mary Lou to hurry up.

"Was that you screaming mommy?" Mary Lou asked, her upper lip draped in the milky substance. Grace felt her own throat close, like her daughters words choked the air she'd been easily breathing just a few seconds before.

"Oh that," Grace began, fumbling for the words as she went along. "That was nothing honey, just stubbed my toe really bad." Becoming self-conscious of her rubber covered hands, Grace ducked them behind her back, praying her daughter wouldn't have any further questions she'd have to lie to answer.

Mary Lou looked down at her mother's foot and Grace instinctively hissed, relaxing her knee and arching her foot to simulate continued discomfort. Mary Lou, seemingly convinced by her mother's charade, finished drinking her milk and sat the glass in the sink.

"Now, off to bed with you, dear," Grace encouraged; ushering her daughter towards the stairs.

"Okay, night mommy." Mary Lou hugged her mother around the midsection and skipped toward the front staircase in her sock covered feet. Grace breathed a huge sigh of relief. Now for the hard part.

Returning to the laundry room, Grace found the dead girl just where she'd left her. Still gloved, Grace took off the trolops' cheap clothes down to her underwear. The whole notion disgusted her but it was a necessary part of the ruse. Grace redressed her in the lacy, ruffly clothes she'd sewn not too many nights before. She managed to pull on the lace trimmed socks. She never knew what size the girl's feet would be; whether the black patent leather shoes would fit snugly or not at all. This time, the size eight shoes were a little big and flopped off the girl's dead feet. Thinking quickly, Grace abandoned the body and went into the kitchen retrieving a few paper towels. She stuffed the toes of the shoes with the paper to provide a snugger fit. The shoes were important. The outfit was not complete without the shoes. Satisfied with the better fit, Grace moved on to the last phase of humiliating her victim.

She painted Tangela's face, obscuring everything that resembled her natural looks; corrupting them with layers of brightly colored paint. Grace had done this before with her own baby doll after her girl abandoned her; leaving Grace in the hands of people who couldn't care for her right. As Grace drew crimson lips on the body, her mind wandered back to those moments she cried for her girl, angered because of the pain she felt; defacing the one thing that reminded her so much of what once was. Grace hated the fact that she loved her girl so much. As she caked on jet black mascara, layering the charcoal substance, Grace felt another surge of uncontrollable anger. Caught in an emotional wave, old pain mixing with new hurt, Grace took the brushed applicator and stabbed at the girl's vacant eyes.

"I hate you, you stupid bitch! Stop looking at me! You don't deserve to look at me you worthless piece of trash!"

Over and over she assaulted the open eyes of the corpse nearly perforating the white of Tangela's eyes, leaving long trails of black ink. Finally, Grace stopped, trying to get her emotions back in check. Grace lifted herself from the floor and placed the mascara applicator back in its case.

Grabbing the girl by the ankles, she dragged Tangela from the laundry room, checking over her shoulder at least one time to make sure her daughter wouldn't disturb her with another surprise visit. They are always heavier than they look, Grace thought, grunting to haul the cargo out into the garage and into the car. Grace disregarded the flat thud she heard as the dead girl's head struck the corner of one wall as she ambled her toward the garage. Once her back was against the door Grace only looked up the length of the girl's body to make sure she hadn't cracked her skull spilling blood on her high polished floors.

Grace allowed the girls' ankle to fall noisily to the floor as she turned and opened the door between the house and the three car garage. Pushing the door and then holding it open with her body, Grace inched the girl over the threshold and onto the concrete slab floor. Fortunately, her 2015 town and country minivan was parked closest to the door. Once the body cleared the kitchen door, Grace released it carelessly, closed the kitchen door and reached into the van to activate the automatic side sliding door.

"All right you black cunt, work with me," she ordered the corpse.

Through trial and error, Grace learned if she got the head and shoulders up and into the vehicle first, the rest of the body was easy to lift in. She hoped that would be the case with this one. The door slid back effortlessly. Grace repositioned herself at the head of the dead girl, bending her knees to lift her to a sitting position. The girl's head flopped lifelessly on a neck that no longer had the wherewithal to hold it upright. Her eyes stood open looking at nothing. Dragging the body closer to the door, Grace stepped inside the van's bed hoisting the corpse's upper body as she went. She tried lifting the body from a semi-standing position. Grace was able to raise the body a few inches but momentarily lost her grip and the girl started to slide the wrong way.

"Dammit... you fuckin bitch... get your ass up here," she scolded the girl who couldn't hear her.

Breathing heavily from near exhaustion and an overabundance of adrenaline, Grace tried it again, this time bending her knees for better leverage. She grunted loudly as the dead weight began to rise from the concrete.

"Come on... come on... come on!"

Grace managed to get enough of the corpse's upper body to clear the bed of the van. Attempting to maneuver around the seat, Grace bent the body unnaturally; pulling the torso further into the van. Dropping the head and shoulders between the seat and the console dividing the captain's chairs, Grace moved to get the rest of the body in. It was necessary to climb into one of the seats to get around the body now blocking her path. Stepping down, teetering on the edge of the van's bed, Grace slipped inadvertently falling forward. She threw up her hands to brace the fall, cursing any and everything in earshot for what the dead bitch made her do. Her concern for whether the children could hear her was the furthest thing from her mind. Grace regained her composure enough to get up and lift the girl's legs into the van. The body was contorted and securely inside, but in order to effectively dispose of the waste Grace knew the importance of getting the body as straight and as close to the sliding door as possible. Pulling from the legs, Grace repositioned the body, rolling the girl on her side to keep the body from interrupting the sliding doors ability to close.

Grace was relieved when she finally depressed the button shutting the door securely behind her. Making her way back into the house, Grace cleaned up any evidence of wrong doing in the laundry room. Grabbing the girl's thrift store clothes, Grace walked into the kitchen, retrieved a small garbage bag and threw them inside. She pushed the bag near the bottom of her kitchen trash bag. Finally relieving her hands of the rubber encasement, Grace scrubbed her own pasty hands under hot water; taking a bristled brush and scrubbing more to eliminate any evidence of leftover blackness that may have penetrated her protection. Wiping her hands on the checkered kitchen towel hung smartly over the sink, Grace picked up the phone. Getting rid of the car was next and she knew just how to handle that.

Chapter Six

Nurse Anna Montgomery reported in to work a few minutes before her shift was scheduled to begin. There was a base level of anxiety that she couldn't shake. It wasn't a bothersome feeling. Quite to the contrary, the low-lying anxious feelings were familiar and bolstered Anna's resolve to effect real change with the patients she would be working with this evening. Anna made a beeline to the pharmacy. She wanted to gauge Ms. Sylvia without the presence of anyone else, just to see how astute she was or wasn't.

"Ms. Sylvia, how are you this fine evening," Anna asked, turning on all her borrowed southern charm.

Sylvia looked up from a novel she was reading and smiled as she saw who stood before her.

"Well, hi there Anna! I see we didn't scare you off yesterday," she jested.

"Of course not," Anna chimed in. "I think I'm going to like Archibald."

"Just stick around Ms. Anna. Before long, you'll love it here like we do!"

Sylvia was the same kind of perky, as long as she was sitting down. Her beehive hairdo seemed even higher today and her ruby red lipstick was bold against her pasty white, wrinkly skin.

"Ms. Sylvia, do you mind if I ask a question," Anna began.

"Not at all honey! Fire away," she encouraged.

"I feel sorta dumb to even have to ask this," Anna began before Sylvia interjected.

"How you gonna know if you don't ask? My mother always said, God rest her soul, the only dumb question is the one you keep to yourself. So ask away honey. If I have the answer, I'll sure give it to you."

"Things were happening kind of fast yesterday when you and Sophie Lynn were talking, but I wanted to find out exactly the procedure to get medications from back there," Anna said innocently enough.

"Well Sugar, you have to have a doctor's order on their prescription pad," Sylvia advised, showing Anna an example of a pad and absentmindedly leaving it on the counter as she continued. "As long as I have one of those on file, then I give the medicine. Without word from the doctor, there ain't much I can do."

"Oh, I see," Anna replied. "And do they write special orders for the medications in the locked box? The only reason I'm asking is because I'll be working with the terminal patients and want to know exactly what I need to get them, exactly what they need." Anna offered a disarming smile in hopes that Sylvia would continue with the details.

"That box stays under lock and key because of the high powered medicines in there," Sylvia said, momentarily turning her back to Anna as she addressed the box on the back wall. Anna had just enough time to swipe the prescription pad and shove it in her smock. "You can still access those medicines with the same note from the doctor!"

Anna placed her arms across the counter, shielding the space where the pad once sat.

"Sylvia, I tell you, you have been most helpful." Anna flashed that award winning smile as Sylvia adjusted herself on the stool. "I better get to the nurses station before they think I'm reporting in late!"

Anna gave a wave and smiled as she left the counter. Sylvia went back to her novel, satisfied that she'd help the new girl. It was only after Sylvia got half way down the page she was reading did she remember something.

"Now where did I put that darn pad?"

Ms. Sylvia spent the next 20 minutes looking for a pad she would never find.

"I was wondering when you'd show up," Nurse Drysdale said as Anna approached the nurses' station. Anna noted a gruff undertone but refused to allow Sophie Lynn to dampen her good feelings.

"Having a bad day Sophie Lynn," Anna asked with her own level of passive aggressive snark.

"Nothing I can't handle," Nurse Drysdale responded dismissively.

"You sure, cause if there's something I can do to help, I certainly will."

"That won't be necessary," Sophie Lynn replied, looking up from her seat behind the rounded countertop. "I'll just be glad when this shift is over and I can start my weekend."

"I hear you," Anna added. "Well, I'm ready when you are."

Nurse Drysdale took her time getting up from the seat and making her way around the counter.

"You can shadow me for the first half of the shift. When I take my lunch, around six, you'll be on your own. Can you handle that?"

"Of course," Anna chirped. Having some alone time played right into her plans for the evening. If Nurse Drysdale was true to how she did rounds the night before, Anna knew she would have the terminal patients to herself for the second half of the shift. She followed closely behind Sophie Lynn but Anna's steps stalled when she saw the direction Nurse Drysdale was going.

"We're doing the terminal wing first?"

"Yes, thought I would get the easy patients out of the way. Do you have a problem with that Nurse Montgomery," Nurse Drysdale snipped.

"Not at all. I'm following your lead," Anna replied; dismissing the curt comment and focusing on the new problem.

"Great. We'll stop by the pharmacy and then be on our way."

Returning to the scene of a crime was never a good idea so Anna had to think quick to avoid what could only be an awkward encounter.

"If it's okay with you, I'll meet you on the wing. Gotta make a pit stop first." Anna squeezed her legs together and made an embarrassed face to demonstrate the urgency of her situation.

"You should have handled that before coming on the floor," Nurse Drysdale quipped, dismissing Anna with a flail of her hand.

Anna didn't doddle. Instead, she headed straight for the employee bathroom where she could think.

Sylvia was still looking for the missing prescription pad when Sophie Lynn arrived.

"Lordy be... if my head wasn't attached to my neck I'd probably forget that too," Sylvia said more to herself than the approaching Sophie Lynn.

"Looks like you're having the kind of afternoon I am," Sophie Lynn commented.

"Just getting so forgetful in my golden years," Sylvia replied with a frustrated laugh. "Maybe when I stop looking for it, I'll find it. What can I help you with Sophie Lynn?"

"The usual," she began. "Handling the terminal patients first tonight."

Sylvia nodded her head and made her way through the pharmaceutical closet filling the order. Nurse Drysdale double checked it for accuracy, considering Sylvia's last statement. She signed off, thanked Sylvia and headed toward the wing she'd be working.

Anna was mindful not to stay too long in the restroom. Sophie Lynn wasn't in the best of moods and Anna didn't want to elevate her rank on Nurse Drysdale's radar. Anna used the time to stash the prescription pad she lifted and to consider how she would handle Sophie Lynn's abrupt change in plans. Anna knew her best chance would be when Nurse Drysdale took her lunch break. She just had to keep it cool until then. Anna figured she could handle that. Flushing the toilet for effect and then a cursory wash of the hands, Anna exited the bathroom; making sure to dispose of the paper hand towels on the outside of the bathroom where her actions would be visible. She had to totally sell it.

Anna met up with Nurse Drysdale just as she rounded the corner towards the terminal wing. All she had to do was bide her time. That's what Anna focused on. Seeing Ms. Jane and Abigail again warmed Anna's heart and reinvigorated her desire to help them along. As they worked room to room, Sophie Lynn remained trite. There was very little commentary about the patients as if Anna needed to have absorbed everything the night before because it wouldn't be repeated. They moved through the first wing so fast, they were well into working with the other patients when six o'clock rolled around.

"Finish up on this wing," Nurse Drysdale directed. "Make sure to write the notes legibly so the doctors can read them... not like we can read a damn thing they scribble on the chart."

Sophie Lynn left Anna in the hallway as she headed towards the employee locker room to retrieve her lunch. Anna was relieved when Sophie Lynn left. She had been a real downer this evening and Anna was excited for what would come next. As she exited the patient's room and headed straight for the employee bathroom, Anna was cautious to make sure she waited long enough so as not to cross paths with Nurse Drysdale. Anna opened the patient's door and peered down the hallway in both directions before stepping out. The bathroom was not far from where she was and fortunately, the hallway showed no sign of Sophie Lynn.

There was someone in the restroom when Anna entered. To avoid looking suspicious, it was necessary for Anna to fake it until the unwanted guest left. She waited until the water from the faucet turned off and the tell-tale sound of paper towels being extracted from the holder before she flushed the toilet, paused a few seconds, and made her exit. The two exchanged smiles as Anna approached the sink to wash her hands. Once the other lady left, Anna walked to the edge of the wall length sink and reached underneath, retrieving the prescription pad. Being tucked under the sink precluded the pad from getting wet. Anna quickly scribbled down the medications she needed, forged a doctor's signature she'd somewhat memorized during rounds and shoved the pad in her pocket. Anna exited the restroom and headed straight for the pharmacy closet.

Ms. Sylvia was still perched on her wooden stool. Anna hurried her breathing as she made her approach.

"Hey there little lady. Got a few scripts to fill before Nurse Drysdale finishes lunch."

"Okey dokey, let me see what you got there," Ms. Sylvia said, grabbing the scripts from Anna's extended hand.

Sylvia looked and then studied the orders.

"These are really hard to read. Who's the doctor?" Sylvia reached for her glasses sitting atop her signature beehive.

"Oh, no need for that Ms. Sylvia," Anna interjected; reaching out and taking the prescription slips from her. "I'll read them to you."

Anna could see Sylvia's mental wheels turning as she considered the offer.

"That's sweet of you dear. It has truly been that kind of day. You read them and I'll cross check to see if I have them on file."

Ms. Sylvia was making this much more difficult than it needed to be. Anna was a quick study, always had been. She just hoped she got enough of the details right so as not to raise alarms with the pharmacist.

"I guess that'll be fine as long as we hurry." Anna made a point of looking at the clock overhead on the hallway wall. "Gotta make sure I get this done before Sophie Lynn finishes up. Don't want to get in trouble on my first solo assignment!"

Anna looked on anxiously to make sure Sylvia understood the urgency with which she spoke. Sylvia nodded her head and Anna began to read off what was on the paper.

"Dr. Boykins ordered tramadol for room 330 and 521... new patients, both of them... in a lot of pain..."

"That Dr. Boykins is one of the worst ones; writing so bad he probably can't even make it out," Sylvia began as she checked the log on the desk in front of her. Anna annoyingly tapped her fingers on the counter. Flustered, by her own absentmindedness and the urgency of the new girl, Sylvia sighed deeply.

"Let me get that for you," Sylvia began, starting to get up from her seat. "I'll cross check it later. If I need you to come back, I'll just call over to the nurses' station."

Anna inwardly felt relieved. At least Sylvia was moving in the right direction. Anna wouldn't be totally satisfied until her angelic deeds were done.

Sylvia was as equally slow moving this time as she had been before. She plodded over to the cabinet, took days it seemed to unlock it and retrieve the prescriptions and then slothfully made her way back. Anna rapped her fingers on the counter, this time out of real impatience.

"All we have left is for you to sign the ledger," Sylvia said, offering Anna a pen. Anna eagerly took it, scribbled her John Hancock on the dotted line, and took the syringes from off the counter where Sylvia sat them.

"Whew, gotta go! Thanks so much Ms. Sylvia," Anna exclaimed as she made a hastened dash from the counter.

"You're welcome dear," Sylvia called after.

Anna knew she didn't have much time. I'm on my way Ms. Jane...

Sophie Lynn separated herself from the other employees in the lounge. She didn't want to have to entertain anyone... didn't want to talk to anyone. Sophie Lynn didn't even want to be at the hospital. So much was going on in her personal life that it severely impacted her mood. Before, Sophie Lynn was able to keep work and home separate, but she was finding it harder and harder. Overhearing other employees laughing and chatting it up only made Sophie angrier. She mindlessly forked her mashed potatoes and Salisbury steak. The blandness of the meal certainly didn't help her mood. If she could only figure out a way to deal with her lazy ass husband. Sophie Lynn was no fool. She acknowledged that times were tough and finding work in a small town could be especially hard, but Luke James wasn't even trying anymore. Sophie Lynn took on extra shifts to cover the bills at home. With three growing boys, the money she made got stretched thinner and thinner.

If he would just get up off his trifling, good for nothing ass and put forth the effort, Sophie Lynn wouldn't be nearly so upset. But when she left for work, he was lying on the couch with his hand wrapped around a beer. No matter what time she arrived home, Sophie Lynn found her husband in the same position. He wasn't even helping with the boys, sticking to the old line of 'that's woman's work'. That's the part that aggravated Sophie Lynn the most. No matter how hard she worked outside the home, she had to come home and work more; dishes overrunning the sink, groceries not purchased, loads of laundry left in mounds still dirty. Luke James wouldn't even throw away the stacks of beer cans he emptied over the course of the day. Too many nights Sophie Lynn stepped on a can, coming in the house without turning on the lights. She stabbed the slab of meat in her plastic Tupperware dish even harder just thinking about it.

Then something else got her attention. The mounted television on the wall had been playing on low in the background. The staff liked to keep the TV on news channels just in case there was something going on that could impact hospital admissions. From where she was sitting and with all the noise in the break room, Sophie Lynn couldn't really make out what the news reporter was saying. It was the picture posted in the background that drew her out of her seat.

"Hush up for a minute," Sophie Lynn exclaimed, raising her voice above the noise. She walked over to the television and turned up the volume. Sophie Lynn was transfixed by what she saw and flabbergasted by what she heard.

"Oh my gawd..."

<hr>

Anna quickly made her way to the terminal wing and found the room she was looking for. As expected, Ms. Jane laid there quietly; well almost quietly. Her breathing was still somewhat labored; as it had been the first time Anna met her. Anna's heart beat at a rapid pace. It was exhilarating. Unlike when she first began helping patients, there was no time for Anna to take Ms. Jane to the brink of death and then be the hero that brought her back from the edge. Anna was a different kind of hero now, helping her patients ease into the afterlife; an existence Anna knew in her heart had to be so much better.

Taking two syringes from her pocket, Anna uncapped the first one and plunged the needle into Ms. Jane's life line. The combination of tramadol and phenobarbital would sufficiently shut down her central nervous system, extinguish any brain activity and stop her heart. Anna smiled widely as she inserted the second needle into the IV line, creating the deadly cocktail in the transparent tube. There was no immediate reaction from Ms. Jane. Anna watched the monitor. Ms. Jane's vital signs were slowing down nicely, and now, the rhythm of her labored breathing became more ragged.

There was a certain level of satisfaction in helping Ms. Jane on her way but the serenity of the kill left Anna feeling woefully dissatisfied. There was only one thing Anna could think of that would make her instantly feel better. She said goodbye to Ms. Jane and made her way to the patient's door. Once opened, Anna made sure to look down both ends of the hallway to ensure the coast was clear. With no one standing in her way, Anna moved to the next room. Two in one night? Anna couldn't remember ever doing that before. Maybe doing two at once would make the sum total a little more exciting.

Although Abigail was also unresponsive, Anna felt a certain thrill with the prospect of ending her life. Because of the things Abigail did, Anna wasn't so sure Abigail's transition would be a beautifully peaceful one. Abigail was a murderer and because of her careless and reckless acts, had taken the life of two innocents, according to the people in town. That in and of itself might be enough to divert Abigail's afterlife path to the pits of hell. At the same time, Abigail was described by

Nurse Drysdale as a victim too; suffering under a lifetime of tragedy at the hands of her mother.

Anna refused to Judge Abigail. As she started to administer the same deadly cocktail she'd just given Ms. Jane, Anna heard ruckus outside the patient's door. Some of the noise Anna expected. The call of code blue echoing in the hallway in response to Ms. Jane's monitor, recording her life flatlining, was a part of any hospital's protocol. What got Anna's attention was the amount of noise she heard. She was nearly tempted to open Abigail's door and look out but proximity to Ms. Jane's room might be a problem. Inadvertently, someone might see her in a place she had no business being. No, Anna would stay the course and fulfill her responsibility.

Anna watched as the medication from the first syringe mixed and mingled in Abigail's tubing. She didn't have to be mindful of bubbles forming in the intravenous line. Death was the desired result so having air bubbles forced into Abigail's veins was like pretty icing on a birthday cake. The noise seemed to be right outside the room Anna was in.

That shouldn't be, Anna thought to herself as she uncapped the second syringe to finalize the lethal cocktail.

When the door to Abigail's room violently swung open, Anna was stunned.

"Hold it right there!" One of the uniformed security guards yelled. Anna had seen him before, nearly sleep on his post. He looked nervous, pointing his taser in her direction.

The second guard stood closely by. Nurse Drysdale made herself visible, stepping from behind the two guards.

"The police are on the way Anna Black," Nurse Sophie Lynn exclaimed. Her eyes were wide and her voice shook a little as she spoke.

"Just let me finish up here," Anna replied, almost too calmly for those in the room with her.

"Put the syringe down Ms. Black, now!" The second security guard yelled as he moved closer to Anna.

"Take her, Bruce," the first guard commanded, lunging in Anna's direction.

"Be careful of that needle," Sophie Lynn screamed, putting a hand to her chest as if her heart hurt.

"Watch her, watch her," Bruce cautioned his partner as they continued to close in on Anna.

"This will only take a minute guys," Anna said smiling back at the guards. She allowed her eyes to find Sophie Lynn. Although the contact between the two women was brief, it was certainly intense. Both smiled but for different reasons. Anna turned her attention back to the most pressing issue. She raised her arm in preparation to insert the syringe. Just then, Anna lost her footing as the second guard, Carl, grabbed her arm, and simultaneously tackled her to the ground, making sure to keep her arm locked so she couldn't use the syringe. Bruce jumped to Carl's aid, doing his best to avoid the needle.

Ahh," Bruce exclaimed as Anna nicked him with the sharp point before Carl was able to wrestle it from her tightly clenched fingers.

"Dammit Bruce! Are you okay," Sophie Lynn asked, moving closer to the commotion now that Anna was subdued.

"Yeah I think so," Bruce replied breathily. "Flip her over Carl and put the zip ties on her," Bruce instructed, trying to ignore the sting from the needle.

The two men sufficiently overpowered the slight Anna and before long, her hands were behind her back and the ties were in place. Both men got up winded and once standing, lifted Anna to her feet.

"We'll keep her in our office until the cops arrive," Bruce said as they passed Sophie Lynn on their way out of the room.

"...sick bitch...," Nurse Drysdale hissed as Anna passed by.

Anna cackled as the two men escorted her down the hallway. Everyone they passed stopped and stared as Nurse Montgomery was ushered along. Ms. Sylvia clutched her fake pearls as Anna was moved passed the pharmacy closet.

"It was nice to meet you Ms. Sylvia!!" Anna jeered as they moved her on.

"What in the world," Ms. Sylvia gasped, not fully understanding what was going on.

"Keep it moving young lady," Bruce insisted. He used the term lady loosely as he thought about the needle prick to his arm.

After leaving the press conference, Dr. Daniels was inundated with telephone calls and other correspondence demanding answers in what appeared to be two serial killer cases; Anna Black who absconded and this new mystery killer, horribly referred to as the baby doll killer.

"I hate when they give them nicknames," Chloe said as she and her assistant rode in the direction of her office.

"This one is especially bad," Addison agreed. "It makes it sound like the murders are not that bad because a doll is associated with it. People tend to have very favorable feelings about dolls. Takes them back to their childhood."

Chloe contemplated what her assistant said. She saw how much Addison had grown, matured and developed as a burgeoning psychologist under her tutelage and Chloe was proud of her development. Maybe there was more to what Addison said than random musings. As Addison expertly navigated through town, Chloe considered linkage and possibilities.

"Defacing the characters sent us in the direction of clowns, but interestingly enough, the moniker was not clown killer," Dr. Daniels thought aloud. "Baby doll killer... the focus was on the doll, not the make-up..."

As Chloe continued to process, the phone rang. Addison answered as Chloe was still deep in thought.

"Dr. Chloe Daniels office, how may I help you?"

Addison listened intently to the caller. What Chloe heard was a series of 'yes, mmhmm, I understand." The call was disconnected and Addison turned the car around.

"What's next on the agenda?"

"County."

"Anna Black?"

"Yes."

Chapter Seven

Anna Black a.k.a. Anna Montgomery was briefly held in the small two-cell jail in Thomasville, Georgia. The chief of police there knew they wouldn't be keeping her long. When the call came in from Archibald Hospital that a woman suspected of several murders was in their midst, Chief Larry Blackpool did two things; dispatched his two officers to the hospital to retrieve the alleged felon, and placed a call to Chief of Police Livingston in Atlanta.

Anna Black was transported to the Atlanta Metropolitan Police Department and placed in custody on one count of murder and one count of attempted murder for her actions at Archibald Hospital. An investigation was launched dating back to her time at Merrill Gardens Senior Citizen Home. Between the combined reports from Merrill Garden, Grady Hospital and now Archibald, Anna faced several additional counts of murder and attempted murder. In cases where Anna Black's patients died on her watch, new autopsies were performed. For those cases that took place early in her reign of terror, permission was gained from family members to exhume the bodies and run the necessary tests to determine if Anna contributed in the death of their loved ones. All of the emergency calls that took place over the months Anna worked at the two medical facilities in Atlanta were scoured and reviewed in an effort to determine the cause.

But that's not why Chloe Daniels was there at the jail. As a forensic psychologist, Dr. Daniels had been called in to try to gain some insight into Anna Black in preparation for the impending trial. From the moment of Anna's arrest up until the time Chloe was called in by the police department, Anna refused to answer any questions. She waived counsel against the advice of her parents and anyone else who tried to caution her. The police hoped Dr. Daniels could breakthrough Anna's wall of silence.

Chloe was no stranger to the jail. She'd been there too many times to count. Before coming down, Dr. Daniels went over all the files and information the police had to offer and dug up whatever background she could find on the elusive Anna Black. Dr. Daniels was intrigued. Clinically, Anna Black was diagnosed as suffering from Munchausen Syndrome with a secondary diagnosis of Munchausen Syndrome by Proxy—an interesting combination to say the least. But according to everyone else's estimation, Anna Black was an Angel of Death.

Even though Dr. Daniels had been in the jail before on similar business, it did not absolve her and her assistant from the standard search to make sure she didn't have any weapons or anything that could be used as a weapon on her person. After the search, Dr. Daniels and Addison were escorted by a guard to the interrogation room where Anna had been moved for the interview. Addison departed from Dr. Daniels and observed the interview through two-way glass. Dr. Daniels thought that best to decrease the number of distractions physically in the interview room.

Upon entering, the doctor noted that Anna didn't bother to look up. Instead, she kept her eyes affixed on the two-way mirror immediately in front of her. Although Addison had only been in the room for a few seconds, she felt Anna's gaze penetrating the glass. It was like the inmate knew someone was there and she was determined to find out who it was. A shiver went down Addison's spine as her eyes met those of the infamous Anna Black. The gaze was chilling, even through thick glass. Anna, dressed in inmate black and white, was humming a tune that was immediately familiar to Chloe after hearing the first few bars.

Dr. Daniels sat down across from Anna and waited a few moments anticipating Anna would finish her song and acknowledge the doctors' presence. Anna continued to hum but her eyes never left the two-way glass. On the other side, Addison, physically took a step back, creating greater distance from her and the assailant, at least in her mind. When Anna continued with her song as if Chloe wasn't there, the doctor cleared her throat.

"Hi Anna, I'm Dr. Daniels."

Anna finished out the chorus before leveling her gaze at Dr. Daniels. Her face creased with an eerily haunting smile. Addison felt a bit of relief when the prisoners' focus was no longer on her.

"Hi Dr. Daniels."

Chloe was somewhat surprised that Anna responded. According to what she'd been told, Anna wasn't saying much of anything to anyone. Maybe she was truly ready to break her silence. Maybe today was Chloe's lucky day. Dr. Daniels decided to press forward to see how far she could get.

"I wanted to talk to you, Anna, about why you're here."

The smile on Anna's face never left and her direct piercing gaze never wavered. It took her a few seconds, but she finally responded.

"I'm here because I helped so many people."

Anna's answer was absolute and frank. She was completely convinced that what she'd done was good. Dr. Daniels would have liked to have been surprised, but she wasn't. She had been doing this job far too long for much to surprise her.

"So you helped Genevieve... George... Stephanie... Drusilla?"

Anna's smile widened.

"Oh Dr. Daniels, I helped a lot more people than that."

Chloe was a bit unnerved. She noted some sociopathic tendencies that up until this point eluded her tentative diagnosis.

"You do know those people are dead now, don't you?"

"But they are in a much better place. Don't you think, doctor?"

Chloe felt a chill move down her spine as Anna spoke.

"Why those people Anna? Why did you help them?"

Again there was a brief silence before Anna responded.

"It's simple... they needed me the most."

Anna sat her bound hands on the table and steepled her fingers. Her affect never faltered.

There was an awkward silence that fell over the room. Dr. Daniels angled for the next question she would ask. She needed to get more from Anna, but Anna was being very guarded. Anna sat waiting for the next inquiry, never flinching.

Their interview was interrupted by a brief knock at the door. Chloe's assistant peeked her head in and signaled she needed to speak with the doctor immediately. Dr. Daniels hated the intrusion, but she could tell by the look on Addison's face that it had to be something major. Addison knew how important this interview was and wouldn't have interrupted her had it not been urgent. She'd been waiting in the lobby for the interview to be over, but when she got the call, Addison knew she couldn't wait any longer.

Dr. Daniels excused herself from the room and stepped out into the hallway. Once the steel door closed behind her superior, Addison leaned in and spoke just above a whisper.

"We've got another body."

Chloe knew exactly what that meant. For now, this interview would be over. There was a much more pressing matter she had to attend to. Dr. Daniels stepped back in the room and spoke to Anna.

"Anna, I'm sorry but I have to end our interview right now. Would it be okay if I came back and talked with you another time?"

Anna gradually turned her head and met the doctor's gaze.

"Of course." Still her menacing smile remained plastered across her otherwise dead face.

As Chloe stepped out of the room, she heard that old familiar tune again.

Hush little baby, don't say a word...

When the phone rang, it cajoled Detective Phillips from the verge of stupor. He'd been working nearly 36 hours nonstop, trying to get ahead of the killer everyone knew he was already behind. Fumbling through the stacks of papers and files on his desk, he retrieved the phone and scrambled to answer it before the caller disconnected.

"Detective Phillips," he answered almost screaming.

"Yes Detective Phillips, this is Amina from the lab."

"Yes, yes... please tell me you got something." His exacerbation was evident in his voice.

"Yes, we did get a hit on one of your victims. Sending over the fax now."

"Thank you."

Detective Phillips sighed heavily after disengaging the call. He crossed the station in record time and stood in front of the fax machine waiting for the beeps to indicate his fax was coming. It seemed like it was taking forever when in all actuality the paper began to generate immediately, inch by inch. He grabbed it out of the machine before it could drop to the catch tray below. Phillips furiously scanned the scant demographic information the fax offered. Most importantly, he now had a name to go with a face. Scrambling back to his desk, he picked up the phone and dialed a familiar number.

"We got a hit," he blurted out barely waiting until she said hello. With that news, Dr. Daniels was willing to overlook the absence of formal salutations.

"You're at the office?"

"Yes."

"I'll meet you there."

Disconnecting the phone, Dr. Daniels advised Addison of the new development.

"Take me to the police station and drop me off. Then you can go to my office and work on Anna's interview."

Dr. Daniels wasn't exactly sure of the full extent of what would happen with the new information Detective Phillips spoke of but it made her hopeful. Whatever it would take to identify the victims to get a better handle on the killer Dr. Daniels was open to. Addison made the necessary adjustments in moving through the city to get her boss to police headquarters. The streets were crowded with afternoon traffic and Addison found it necessary to maneuver through side streets to bypass some of the gridlock.

When Dr. Daniels entered the police station and then the bullpen where Detective Phillips worked, she could see from across the room he was anxiously awaiting her arrival as he paced back and forth like a caged animal, staring down at what she assumed was the new information. Sensing her presence, he turned mid-pace and looked in her direction. Michael fought the instinctual inclination to smile as though seeing a long lost lover although he felt that way. She was a breath of fresh air with her effortless beauty and poise. Refocusing, Detective Phillips shook away the amorous images and greeted her professionally.

"Dr. Daniels," Detective Phillips offered, trying desperately to keep his intonation flat and unassuming.

"Detective Phillips," Dr. Daniels replied, sitting her purse and briefcase down in the chair nearest his desk. "What do we have?"

Michael positioned himself alongside Chloe in order to share the fax he'd received. Dr. Daniels scanned the information quickly, recognizing the face of their second victim. There was her name. For the first time she wasn't a Jane Doe. Her name was Dominique Sanders. The missing person report had a date, December 17, 2012. That's when those who knew Dominique Sanders notified the authorities she was missing.

"What's your course of action detective?"

The two separated and Michael took the seat behind his desk. Chloe removed her belongings from the chair and sat in the seat beside the desk.

"I waited until you got here to make the call," Detective Phillips responded pointing to the contact number near the bottom of the page.

"Well, let's make the call."

Detective Phillips took out his cell phone and dialed the number. The party on the other end of the phone answered on the third ring.

"This is Detective Moore, how can I help you?" Michael was a bit surprised to hear a woman's voice on the other end of the phone.

"Yes, this is Detective Michael Phillips with the Atlanta Police Department. We got a hit on a missing person."

The two detectives continued to converse, exchanging and securing information. Dr. Daniels was only privy to bits and pieces of the information but could tell from the notes Detective Phillips jotted down that he was getting closer to determining some of the most pertinent facts about the case. She could hardly wait when he disconnected the call to find out what he learned. Seeing her anxious expression, Detective Phillips didn't hesitate.

"It looks like we have an Atlanta connection. If we get to her early enough we may be able to make South Carolina before night fall. You up for that?"

"Absolutely," Dr. Daniels replied, getting up from the seat and grabbing her bag. "Let's go."

The tow truck Grace called arrived at 8:30 p.m. just in enough time to have the car removed before Drake was slated to arrive. She'd called the service advising that an unknown vehicle had been parked in front of her home all day and she demanded it be removed. Few questions were raised given the neighborhood and the Wetherby's station in life. That part of the problem out of the way, Grace turned her attention to receiving her husband. It was always a delicate dance. She loved Drake and hated him for what he'd done. Had she not loved him at some base level she would've enacted her revenge on him directly. But he was the father of her children. They loved him as only children could. She couldn't do that to them although she thought about it.

Drake arrived a few minutes after nine. Grace greeted him with a strong drink and lukewarm dinner. He downed them both in record time. They briefly discussed the events of the day, some of them. Although Preston was feeling somewhat better, Grace made sure to convey just how sickly he'd been. Preston would be her excuse to get out of the house and dispose of the body. Drake pushed back from the table promising to check on Preston. He would at some point, Grace was sure of that, but not before he relaxed in the bottom of a fifth of hard liquor. That was just fine with her. The duller his senses the less she would have to explain. He was so preoccupied with getting to his drink, he didn't bother to inquire about the help she'd hired earlier in the day. He knew better...

She waited until he'd been in the library a few hours and made his way to the master bedroom. Grace visited Mary Lou's room and found her sound asleep. Preston's room was next door. He seemed to be sleeping well. Going into her bedroom, she told Drake she needed to run out for a minute to pick up some medicine for Preston. He was unresponsive; too inebriated to care she suspected. Her informing Drake was just a formality. If he'd protested she still would have left. She had to. The body in her van wouldn't wait until the next day.

Grace stepped into her closet making sure to put on a dark shirt. She grabbed her black scarf and exited the bedroom. Drake rolled over and grunted.

No matter how early or how late it was, there was traffic on Atlanta highways. Grace knew there was always a chance someone would see her; the chance she would be caught in the act. That's part of what added to the excitement. Grace drove through the city trying to determine the best place to go. Her last dump spot was hot, too hot to return to, at least right now. She'd find another obscure location, far enough away from home but not too far that it would take her an exorbitant amount of time to get back, just in case Drake came back to his senses.

Downtown Atlanta was not only the epicenter of the city but it also provided the interstate connectors she needed to find her next location. Taking a right and veering off the 75/85 exchange, Grace scouted for an overpass on highway 20. This would be the perfect location as most of the folks who lived in and around that area were just like the coon she was dropping off. There was some traffic but it was lighter than expected. That pleased Grace. About eight miles in of naked road with no overpass, Grace took a left where the interstate split into highway 285 and Martin Luther King Jr. Drive. How fitting, she thought, to drop off one jigaboo on the road named for the spook who tried in vain to save them. She found her spot. Grace put on the hazard lights and slowed the truck down to a crawl before stopping on the MLK side. She checked her rearview mirror to make sure all was clear before putting the remote side door into action; rolling it back.

The area was dark with the exception of a few cars speeding by. Grace, partially hooded with her black scarf covering her ashy blonde hair, hopped the arm of the captain's chair. Grace was ready to rid her van of today's garbage. Just then, the van was suddenly awash with the signature red and blue lights from a police vehicle. Grace's heart leapt in her throat and beat hard against her rib cage. She didn't know if the cop saw her moving to the back of the vehicle, but Grace immediately got back in the drivers' seat, slamming her finger repeatedly against the button to close the side door.

"Come on, come on, please close, please close."

Grace was nearly panic stricken as she watched the officer exit the patrol car and walk toward her. The closer he got, Grace realized the officer was Black. She rolled her eyes to the top of her head. ...poetic fuckin' justice, she contemplated as the nigger officer made his presence known. She tried every trick in the book to calm herself; her nerves now peppered with resentment. When the officer rapped on her window, instructing her to lower it, Grace prayed silently to a God she hadn't spoken to in years while simultaneously attempting to mask her disgust.

"Yes, officer, is everything okay?" Grace offered with a nervous smile.

"Drivers' license and registration ma'am," the officer replied dryly.

"Okay, no problem, but is everything alright?" He didn't respond. Grace didn't appreciate his curtness but she was in no position to protest.

Grace needed to know the answer to the question she raised. She needed to gauge just how much trouble she was in.

"My purse is behind my seat. Is it okay if I reach back to get it," Grace asked. She didn't want the officer to become suspicious of anything she did. She knew how they could be. Turning away from him to reach behind her may give the officer a reason to do something rash. Grace didn't want that. When the cop nodded his approval of her movement, she politely thanked him and it sickened her a little.

"Slowly," the officer directed. He couldn't see the face Grace made as she turned away from him.

Being overly cautious, Grace left one hand visible for the officer to see and reached behind the captain's chair with her right hand. She grabbed her purse by the strap and slowly lifted it high so the officer could see what it was. Sitting the purse in her lap, Grace fumbled for her wallet, eventually finding it and securing the items the officer requested. As the officer illuminated her identification with his flashlight, Grace shifted in the captain's chair to keep the light from illuminating the garbage lying by the side door.

"Just a moment, I will be right back," the officer advised.

Grace waited until she saw the car door open. She looked over toward the door to see just how much of the help was visible. Fortunately, not much could be seen from her vantage point. Grace just hoped against hope the officer couldn't see anything from where he had been standing.

"...fuck...fuck...fuck..."

Nothing Grace could do slowed her racing heart. The echo in her ears was nearly deafening. What was taking him so long? Probably incompetent...What did she do to warrant being pulled over? Endless scenarios played in Grace's mind as to what could happen next. She repeatedly checked the rearview mirror for movement as highway traffic continued to whiz by. Seconds ticked by like minutes and minutes like hours. Finally, there was movement. Grace watched the officer as he approached the back of her vehicle. He stood there for a second and Grace considered maybe there was something back there drawing his attention. Fuck, fuck, fuck...

When he moved toward the driver's side door, there was a moment when the air filling Grace's lungs felt cut off. She was near hyperventilation waiting to see what the spook had to say. Grace could barely contain herself and her words assaulted his ears before he had a chance to speak.

"Officer, everything okay?" Grace's words were choppy and disconnected as her thoughts raced.

"I pulled you over because you failed to signal," the officer replied flatly.

A gust of hot air escaped her lips as Grace breathed a sigh of relief. She considered correcting him; telling the officer that there was no one immediately behind her that she needed to signal for. But, given her present situation, Grace thought better of it. The officer returned her identification and Grace quickly shoved it in her purse, not bothering to place it back in her wallet. The officer halted her action as Grace presumptuously began to roll the window back up.

"Ma'am," he asserted.

"Yes?"

"Here's your citation. You have a right to appeal. The fine and the court date are listed on the ticket."

"You're giving me a ticket?"

"Have a good evening ma'am."

Grace reluctantly took the ticket from the officer's hand, minding not to touch him in the process. She cursed him as he walked back to his patrol car. Grace was seething. Throwing her purse behind her, Grace put the minivan in gear. She made sure to put her blinker on, slamming the arm down into position. When the officer didn't pull out from behind her, Grace considered what he was waiting for. Probably waiting to fine me for something else... bastard...

Grace minded her p's and q's as she looked behind her before pulling out onto the highway. It was only after she was enroute did the officer leave the side of the road and pull out behind her. He had completely derailed her plans and now Grace had to backtrack and find a new location to dump the body. She made sure to drive under the speed limit; not to draw any additional undo attention to herself. She had to work her way back downtown, back to a high traffic area and an overpass to get rid of the trash. Grace made the decision to exit highway 285 on Camp Creek, reenter on the other side and take highway 20 back to the interchange. That was her best bet for a successful dump. At some point, she lost the officer behind her and Grace, although still pensive, felt a little more at ease. She just had to drive, execute and go home. That was it.

Traffic on interstate 20 had thinned to some degree. It took Grace less time to get back to the interchange then her original trip. Within minutes, Grace was back where the highways merged and on highway 85. This time she was extremely careful, making sure to put her blinker on as she approached the overpass she decided to dump under. Once the car was securely to the side of the road, Grace put the car in park and then waited. She watched out of her rearview mirror, waiting to see if she had unwanted company; whether officer Bob would find himself behind her again. None came. She retraced her previous actions, clicking the button to open the side door, and climbing out of the captain's chair to access the body. With another cursory look around, Grace moved. With one swift kick, the body was disengaged from her vehicle. Grace barely paid attention to the thud the body made as it hit the pavement; most of the sound drowned out by the noise from traffic. Grace didn't look back as she climbed pack into the driver's seat and engaged the button, closing the side door. Success...

Within minutes, Grace was on her way home. She smiled but it didn't last. Successful execution of the drop-off was as close to the downside of the kill as Grace got. Almost all the thrill was gone with the exception of the memories.

She always remembered the most important part; not their name or any distinguishing physical characteristic. To Grace, they all looked the same. She remembered the kill – overtaking them and bending them to her will. She would hunt again and soon. Grace didn't see movement on the side of the road; creeping out from the shadowed covering of the overpass. But he saw her and what she left behind.

Chapter Eight

Grace crawled in bed. He rolled over. The smell of cognac was heavy on his breath. He started to kiss her. Grace turned her face and his thin, drunk, stained lips landed on her cheek. Drake pressed his body against her. It had been far too long since he'd been with his wife. He missed her. He was still trying to get things back on track. He'd cheated before but not under her nose. Drake needed to get back on solid ground with his wife the best way he knew how. Grace recoiled from his touch. She missed him too in that way but her anger blinded her physical inclinations. Drake was persistent. He groped her breasts reaching through her thin nightgown. She felt his hardness pressing against her buttocks. Her body began to betray her; moistening in places that had been dry and barren. He felt her body starting to give and climbed on top of her, rolling her over to face him. The promise of pussy was blinding and Drake clumsily lifted her gown over her knees and pressed her legs open. Grace's mind overrode her body.

"Get off me Drake..."

He started to beg, persistent in parting her jewel box.

"Drake get off me..."

Physically Grace was no match for Drake, but given his condition and the anger that lied just beneath the superficial surface, Grace pushed him. In the darkened room, her hands landed on his face but Grace didn't care. He swatted her hands down; harder than he intended. He just wanted to love her and she was making it difficult. Grace reared up, pushing against whatever part of him she could find; his chest, his arms.

"You fucked that skank black bitch in my bed! You'll never touch me again! Get the hell off me Drake, I mean it..."

Frustrated, Drake relinquished, crawling off his wife and retreating to his side of the bed.

"You need to get over it," Drake moaned, his voice partially muffled by the pillow.

"You should have fuckin' kept your dick in your pants," Grace snarled, turning her back to him. She was more resolved than ever. Someone was going to pay.

Detective Phillips and Dr. Daniels made their way to what they hoped would be a significant clue in the chain necessary to find their killer. Michael drove, easily moving through the city streets. He knew these roads like the back of his hands having been a law enforcement officer in the area for nearly eight years. Chloe had a lot on her mind. She was hopeful this trip would not be in vain. She contemplated the days' events as she peered out of the passenger side window. The pressure was mounting and Chloe hoped resolution to this case would come sooner than later.

There was a pleasant tension in the car; neither of the two having too much to say to each other directly. Michael determined to stay focused.

Being in such close and closed physical proximity with Chloe was difficult. Her signature scent, although subtle, entranced him, making it difficult for Michael to stay as focused as he intended. Chloe sensed the tension too. It had been like that between the two since they'd first met. She had a sense Michael wanted their relationship to be more than what it was. He'd made a shallow attempt over a year ago but nothing since then. Maybe she'd been too direct with him about her need to focus on the job. Maybe he'd been discouraged by it. Chloe didn't think that to be completely true. She noted the stolen glances and had to admit she'd stolen a few of her own. Chloe smiled as the self-realization played out in her mind. She turned her head even further toward the window to keep Michael from seeing it.

4576 McClendon Ave NE in Candler Park was their destination and Detective Phillips found a parking space near the front of the residence. The house faced the park and there was a host of activity; people walking their dogs, children playing, all seeming to enjoy the late afternoon sun. Detective Phillips exited the vehicle and made his way around to the passenger side. He opened the door for Dr. Daniels and she nodded her head noting his gentlemanly tendencies typically reserved for a date. This was far from it but she didn't hold his manners against him. The two mounted the stairs and Detective Phillips rang the doorbell.

It took a few moments for the resident to answer. When the door opened the resident looked perplexed by the strangers standing at her door.

"Can I help you?"

Detective Phillips flipped his badge letting the resident know the visit was official. "And this is Dr. Daniels," Phillips offered. "She's a consultant for the police department."

"Are you April Griffin?" The resident nodded her head affirmatively. "We need to speak to you about Dominique," Detective Philips said, taken one step closer to the entrance. April stepped aside and allowed the strangers to enter her home. She led them to the living room where they all took a seat. Dr. Daniels, as was her nature, quietly observed her surroundings, learning as much about the resident by what she saw as by what she would soon hear.

"Is Dominique okay?"

April asked, pulling her legs up in the chair she sat in. She was dressed casually in a tee shirt and jeans. Her feet were bare. She was comfortable in her own home. April didn't seem as comfortable in her own skin; however, fidgeting and adjusting, running her hands through her braided hair in anticipation of the strangers' response.

"When was the last time you saw Dominique?" Detective Phillips skillfully dodged the question; rather, insisting on forwarding his investigative agenda.

"It's been a few months, can't say for sure," April replied, readjusting in her seat once again. "But you didn't answer my question detective. Is Dominique okay?"

The fact that he hadn't answered gave April pause and she found it more and more difficult to keep the feeling of doom cascading over her at bay.

She deserved an answer and Phillips intended to give it to her. He needed more from her though.

"What was the nature of her visit?" Detective Phillips pressed on, noting her growing agitation.

April rolled her eyes, not trying to keep her disdain for the detectives' insistence a secret.

"I'm not answering one more question sir until you answer mine. Is Dominique okay?" April's voice was elevated and Dr. Daniels could see her increased anxiety level. She understood Phillips tactics but it wasn't fair to April. She leveled her gaze at him, signifying the importance of resolving the angst for this woman. He felt Dr. Daniels looking at him as he kept his eyes on the witness. He didn't want to risk alienating her completely.

"I'm sorry to say Dominique is not okay, Ms. Griffin. That's why we're here."

"Well where is she? Is she in the hospital or something?"

"No ma'am…"

There was an awkward pause. Phillips hated delivering this kind of news but in his line of work it was inevitable. April became more frantic even before he said the fateful words.

"What... what are you saying, sir... what are you saying?"

"I'm sorry to inform you ma'am but Dominique is dead."

Dead... the word hung in the atmosphere like a low dark thunder-filled cloud. Dr. Daniels watched April as she heard it; not sure if she was processing it, but she definitely heard it. April's mouth was agape. Her eyes were wide. She didn't, possibly couldn't speak. Phillips dared not press forward. This was a delicate moment and he recognized it as such.

April's face contorted before the tears started to fall. Detective Phillips dropped his head not wanting to bear witness to her sorrow. April cried quietly and undisturbed for a few moments. Between tearful spurts she repeated, "I can't believe this... I just can't believe this." Phillips waited until the crying dissipated.

"Were you not surprised you hadn't heard from her?" His voice was gentler, less forceful than it had been before.

"No," April responded, wiping tears from her eyes. "It's not like we talked every day or every week. So when I didn't hear anything I thought everything was fine." It was hard for her to speak as her sorrow continued to spill over.

"What did she come here for?" Dr. Daniels inquired.

"She needed a change..."

"A change?"

"Yeah, she felt suffocated by her momma. They were getting into it all the time. She wanted a change so she came here to see how it was in the big city, to see if she could find a job and move up here permanently."

"How long did she stay with you?"

"She was here a couple of three weeks." April chuckled. "The first week or so we partied hard," she laughed again. "We really did, but after a while she got serious and started looking for work."

"What kind of work was she looking for?" Detective Phillips asked.

"Whatever she could find. Dom only has... I mean had a high school diploma so she looked for whatever she could get."

April shook her head, realizing her friend could no longer be referred to in present tense.

"Did she find anything?"

"I can't really say. Near the end of her stay with me we kind of got into it. You know, two grown women in the house together... there's bound to be some conflict. I hate knowing that the last time I saw her we were at odds like that." April paused reminiscently and then continued.

"She started to feel herself after she got an interview for a housekeeping job. She had it all planned out what was going to happen, how she was going to be making her own money and wouldn't need anybody... that's how the argument started. She made me feel like she was taking advantage of me, not appreciating what I'd done for her. It's stupid now that I think about it." April's look was somber. It was evident she was still reeling from the impactful news.

"I know this is difficult Ms. Griffin and we certainly appreciate how cooperative you've been. I just have one more question. Did she give you any inclination as to who she was going to work for?"

April was tired now. Her energy was drained from the emotional low experienced at the hands of the detective.

"She never said specifically. All she said was it was a rich white woman."

It wasn't much to go on but it was all April had to give them. Detective Phillips and Dr. Daniels thanked her for her time.

"Can you remember the last day you saw her or talked to her?" April paused for a long time. They could almost see her calculating in her head trying to come up with an answer.

"This is June right?" Dr. Daniels nodded her head.

"Okay... she came here at the end of February I think. The last time I talked to her or saw her was around the second week of March. I can't say what day... just that that's the day we fell out."

"Did she leave anything here?" Detective Phillips inquired.

"She didn't come here with much, just a duffle bag with some clothes and stuff in it. She took it the day we argued. I can't say she left anything of any importance. What little scraps she may have left around, I know I've thrown away by now." The somber and distant look returned to April's face. Dr. Daniels looked at Phillips and he stood up. It was time to go. April fell in behind them escorting them back to the front door.

"If you think of anything else or if you find anything at all she may have left that might help with the investigation Ms. Griffin, please don't hesitate to call." Phillips extended a business card as the two descended the front stairs. Once back in the car, they debriefed regarding the interview.

"Dammit!" Detective Phillips frustration showed as he slammed the car door.

"What's bothering you?"

"It's not enough, what she gave us is not enough."

"She did the best she could Michael. You can't fault her for that," Dr. Daniels responded, turning and fastening her seatbelt.

"I know. It's just..." Worry lines creased his forehead. Chloe could appreciate the pressure he was under.

"Hey," she began. Michael looked in her direction, the fret on his face failing to relax.

"We'll make it happen just like we did before."

She was right. They had worked through an incredibly tough case with as little insight as this one and came out on the winning end with the suspect locked away for his eternity. Michael's worry lines relaxed a bit and he offered Chloe a bit of a smile.

"Now we just have to put the rest of the pieces together."

With that, Michael buckled up, turned over the ignition and put the truck in gear. Next stop? South Carolina. The two set out for the three hour ride. Notifying the family of Dominique's' demise was the part they were least looking forward to. They could only hope they'd learn enough to get the investigation moving in the right direction.

Addison knew she needed to come through for Dr. Daniels. Things had been hectic before but with the two cases happening simultaneously, the demands from the police department as well as the prosecuting attorney's office, her boss was being pulled in too many directions. If she could help with the Anna Black case to get the recommendations to the prosecuting attorney, then maybe some of the weight would be lifted from Dr. Daniels shoulders.

Addison always enjoyed working in Dr. Daniels home office. She was never still long enough to have a traditional office so she used her home as headquarters for all the work she did. It worked out well. When things got hectic, as they often did, Chloe could go from work to leisure by just turning a few corners. On those occasions when it was necessary for Addison to work late, there was a spare bedroom where she could crash when it was too late to cross town and return to her small efficiency apartment. As much as Addison knew about Dr. Chloe Daniels, she felt like there was still so much more she didn't know. Chloe's home offered some insight as to the two sides of her – the professional side and the personal side.

Dr. Chloe's office was austere, streamlined with very few if any frills. Cool colors in muted blues and greens offset by chrome accents provided the backdrop for the intellectual work that took place within the offices confines. Immediately outside the office is where the difference began. The color scheme, although complimentary, was intensified. The blues and greens and grays were much more pronounced; providing a lively, eye-catching yet quirkily serene landscape. Her décor was complex yet simplistic with clean lines and minimalistic clutter, more like purposed groupings that caused the eye to pause, take it in and move on to the next collection of interesting things.

Instead of working in the office, Addison decided to work in the family room sitting cross-legged in front of the coffee table. Before her lay everything she knew about the Anna Black case including files, notes, recordings and court transcripts. First on the agenda was to tackle the most recent interview. Although the other items would be helpful in 'profiling' the suspected killer, they were only part and parcel to what could be used to review and grade the interview. Addison used the Diagnostic and Statistical Manual of Mental Disorders, DSM-IV; a widely used manual for diagnosing mental and behavioral disorders, to determine the most appropriate tentative clinical diagnosis for Anna Black. In order to provide the most appropriate diagnosis, Addison had to review the criteria and align the interview with the noted qualifiers. It was difficult to not allow her personal impression of the woman to cloud her clinical judgment. Just remembering the sadistic intense look that bore through her soul was enough to elevate goose bumps on her arm that had barely subsided since the initial encounter. Shaking her head to rid herself of the creepy memory, Addison refocused on the task in front of her. Of course, Dr. Daniels would have the final say as to the diagnosis presented to the prosecuting attorney and the court, but Addison understood the importance of the preliminary work.

Combing through the scholarly literature was no easy feat but Addison landed on a tentative diagnosis she felt could be on target. The big book of all things psychologically disturbing offered a definition for what Anna's interview manifested. "...defines antisocial personality disorder as a pervasive pattern of disregard for and violation of the rights of others occurring since age fifteen, as indicated by three (or more) of the following:

1. Failure to conform to social norms with respect to lawful behaviors as indicated by repeatedly performing acts that are grounds for arrest;

2. Deceitfulness, as indicated by repeated lying, use of aliases, or conning others for personal profit or pleasure;

3. Impulsivity or failure to plan ahead;

4. Irritability and aggressiveness, as indicated by repeated physical fights or assaults;

5. Reckless disregard for safety of self or others;

6. Consistent irresponsibility, as indicated by repeated failure to sustain steady work or honor financial obligations;

7. Lack of remorse, as indicated by being indifferent to or rationalizing having hurt, mistreated, or stolen from another.

Addison perused the list. Immediately there were some factors that stood out to her. From the social history Dr. Daniels derived from interviewing Anna's parents, teachers, classmates and co-workers, pieces of her life that bespoke how deeply rooted her psychosis was were evident. Even from a child there was something a little 'off' about Anna. Addison rummaged through the material on the make-shift desk. Once before she'd scanned the information but now she needed to read it in earnest. After shuffling and restacking a few piles, she found what she was looking for. It was an in-person interview Dr. Daniel's conducted with Mrs. Black, Anna's mother, not long after Anna was first arrested and charged with several counts of murder in the first degree.

Things were fine with Anna. She's always been a bright little girl and we doted on her because she was so precarious. I hate to admit it but it was my own selfish desire that changed things. Had I been satisfied with the great life God had given me, I know none of this would've happened. My husband tried to turn me against the idea of having another baby, especially at my age, but my heart had room enough for one more. I never intended to make any difference between my children because I love them both the same. It's just that Angel was a certain kind of special and her care demanded so much of our time and attention. By the time Angel came along Anna was a big girl and pretty self-sufficient so I probably depended on her more and more to take care of the little things I felt she could manage herself. There's nothing wrong with gaining independence, is there?

Anna started getting sickly behind her sister being so sick. It was just minor stuff, you know, a stomachache here and there at first but it started to escalate to the point that Anna tried to take her own life. That frightened me... it really did, but I still didn't put the pieces together like I should. I have to admit I was overwhelmed, Tom was overwhelmed; we were drowning trying to take care of Angel. We had help, true enough, but the bulk of her care fell on us. The guilt I felt for her condition and the guilt I felt for having her even when the doctors and my husband tried to talk me out of it, I think it kept me from being able to see the pain I was causing. I was too busy being hyper-vigilant about Angel; wanting to be supermom; not wanting to burden them and making it out like I could handle it even when my heart was breaking. It seemed like there was one crisis with Angel after another and because of my singular focus, the crises with Anna just didn't rise to the level they should have. By that time, Peter completely checked out. He was disgusted with the whole situation and with me...

When I learned of some of the other things she'd put herself through, the cutting and the starving herself, I just couldn't wrap my mind around it. It was so not like the Anna I knew. Asking Anna to help with her sister, though, may have pushed her in a way she didn't want to be pushed. It was only after this stuff started coming out that I thought back to those earlier times; times when things would happen with Angel that were odd. We always just chalked them up to her medical condition, she has several. She would take a turn for the worse or maybe just a weird quirk from the medication she was on, we just thought it was par for the course. I refused to believe that some of the things she suffered were at the hand of her sister. Still have a hard time believing that now...

Addison scanned the pages, looking for diagnostic feedback from early in Anna's life. There was none. The brief encounter she had with a social worker after trying to commit suicide offered nothing more than a curt glimpse into what was most likely going on with Anna at the time. Dr. Daniel sketched some notes and Addison reviewed them. Munchhausen syndrome... based on Anna's early self injurious behavior. But the diagnosis shifted somewhere and Anna's attention seeking, self-mutilating behaviors turned outward, morphing into something else. Dr. Daniels noted the change indicating Munchhausen syndrome by proxy; a conditioning not recognized by the DSM-IV. Rather, this specific condition was defined as factitious syndrome by proxy.

Deception is at the core of the proxy diagnosis and fit Anna to a tee, whether she acknowledged it or not. But there was another metamorphosis with the infamous Anna Black when she became the Angel of Death. Addison spent the rest of the evening listening again to the interview, cringing as she'd done before at the hearing of Anna's eerie voice.

There was another layer to Grace's story she dared not consciously admit to. She had a girl. When she was young growing up in Old Man Pembroke's home, she too had a girl that she loved. Grace hated herself for that. Despite everything her father said about niggers not being good for shit, Grace had fallen in love with Miriam. She was their housekeeper and Grace's primary caregiver from as early as Grace could remember. Nellie Wayne Pembroke, Grace's mother, was sickly and bedridden. She couldn't provide the kind of care a young girl needed. When Grace was older, she would visit with her mother, sit by her bedside and watch her sleep or writhe in pain. Grace was never able to stay too long. The adults in her life didn't want her to see her mother suffering that way. Explaining the kind of sickness Nellie had was hard and Grace wasn't to be burdened with that. That's where Miriam came in. She more than filled in the gap for Nellie and took care of Grace like she was her own.

Miriam left abruptly when Grace was ten years old. Grace was devastated. She loved Miriam like the mother she longed for. Old Man Pembroke offered no explanation. He just said the bitch was worthless and she had to go. The only thing Grace had left of Miriam outside of memories was a little black doll Miriam left her. Grace cried with that doll, played with that doll, hated the doll, took out her frustrations on that doll, she missed Miriam so. Years later, Grace learned the truth about Miriam's departure. The love Grace had for Miriam as a child instantly turned to hate. Grace shook her head, attempting to rid herself of the pained memories. She had more immediate matters requiring her attention.

Chapter Nine

He lurked in the shadows. Nobody ever saw him. To society, he was invisible. But he'd seen her, the white woman trying to hide who she was. The beam from an oncoming car had given just enough light for him to catch a glimpse of her. He saw what she did too. The man ventured from his home, out from the protection of the shadows and security the overpass provided to get a closer look at what was left.

***

The ride to South Carolina was peppered with times of great conversation and long pauses of what could have been awkward silence. Chloe was surprised at just how easy it was to talk to Michael, especially about subjects not directly related to the job. He was well versed in areas she found unexpected; having previously pigeon-holed him into the typical tough guy role, absent culture and substance. He was more than that she learned. Chloe smiled slyly, gazing out of the window taking in the sights. Maybe she'd judged him too harshly, not willing to give him a chance when he'd let on that he was interested in getting to know her on a personal level. Chloe had to admit to herself there were moments when she felt utterly alone; absent attention and affection from a man. She'd busied herself over the past few years with establishing her career and fighting to make a name for herself. Chloe had long since neglected her personal life and most recently began to feel the tangible effects of that neglect.

The ride had been equally enjoyable for Michael. Although it wasn't the kind of alone time he so desperately craved with the beautiful Chloe, it would have to do for now. He could tell she was more relaxed around him, not as uptight as she seemed whenever they were working. Even though this was still work, maybe the open road or the distance from the city and all that brought to bear caused her new disposition. Whatever it was Michael liked it and hoped to see more of it.

Nearing their destination, Chloe refocused the conversation to the situation at hand.

"Do you know if the detective in South Carolina notified the mom?"

"No she didn't. Detective Moore wanted to wait until we arrived before notification," Michael replied as the navigation system alerted to the distance to their destination.

"I can't even imagine... this mom has no idea what's about to happen," Chloe commented. She didn't have children of her own but she'd lost loved ones close to her. That pain was great, but no parent, no mother, expects to have to bury their child.

"Yeah, she has no idea."

Michael pulled out his cell phone and contacted Detective Moore to notify of their position. She agreed to meet them at the victim's mothers' house.

Hush

The rest of the ride was somber and quiet. Soon Detective Phillips and Dr. Daniel's pulled up to 112 Jebedie Road. The shotgun house was a pale shade of gray with an even darker roof. The small porch was just big enough for a single gliding chair. The white rail encasing the porch was chipped and almost barren, fading into the backdrop. The house looked sad but there was one bright spot. Wrapped around the trunk of a small tree in the front yard was a yellow ribbon; drooping now from too many sunny and rainy days in the South Carolina weather.

Detective Phillips pulled up behind the midnight blue cruiser a few feet from the front of the house. He grabbed the envelope that held the victims' picture. A woman dressed in a dark suit climbed out of the cruiser just as Detective Phillips opened the door for Dr. Daniels.

"Detective Moore?" Phillips asked, closing the door and rounding the front of the vehicle.

"Yes, good to meet you Detective Phillips. Wish it was under better circumstances," Detective

191

Fatima Moore responded, extending her hand and giving Phillips a hearty shake.

"This is Dr. Chloe Daniels," Phillips advised placing his hand at the small of Chloe's back. "Dr. Daniels is a forensic psychologist working with us on this case."

The two women greeted each other cordially.

"Are you familiar with the residents?"

"Yes, I've been out here a time or two," Detective Moore explained. "Had a few disturbance calls but nothing major until this."

They advanced towards the door. The rickety porch stairs creaked as the threesome made their ascent. Detective Moore stood slightly ahead and rapped on the screen door. Chloe could hear music coming through a partially cracked window near the front of the house. Detective Moore knocked again when there was no response.

"Coming, I'm coming," a woman's voice replied from inside the house. A few seconds later the front door opened. Her cheery disposition quickly changed when she saw the grouping on her porch. One she recognized, the others she didn't.

"This can't be good all ya'll here together this time of evening."

She wiped her hands on an apron draped on the front of her dress and pushed the screen door open. There was no exchange of greetings as that seemed inappropriate given the circumstances. The three officials walked in and waited for direction on where to go. The woman of the house left the main door opened and ushered the group into the living room. Before she sat, she made a point of turning down the music that had been playing in the background. It was Mahalia Jackson's "Troubles of the World".

"Tell me why ya'll are here," she replied looking directly toward the familiar, Detective Moore. "Don't sugar coat it. I don't have the energy for sugar coating."

The woman was older than Dr. Daniels anticipated; her hair graying at the temples, her dark brown face tired and worn.

"I won't sugar coat it for you Ms. Robinson," Detective Moore began. "We're here because of Dominique."

Ms. Robinson never dropped her gaze. She continued to look towards Detective Moore in anticipation. She was patting her foot, faster, and with more intention. There was no sound from the patting as her feet were covered in well-worn house slippers. The sound of Mahalia's powerfully melodic voice filled in the gaps in conversation, offering a stirring backdrop to the sadness of the moment.

"Well, I can tell from how ya'll looking that it ain't good."

She was strong. By looking at her, Dr. Daniels could tell that over the course of her life she'd had to be strong even when she may have felt otherwise. Ms. Robinson had the look of someone who'd seen too much too soon.

"No ma'am, it's not good," Detective Phillips interjected.

"This is Detective Michael Phillips and Dr. Daniels from Atlanta, Ms. Robinson," Detective Moore offered.

"Is that where they found her?" Ms. Robinson's face began to distort but she quickly brought it back to flat as best she could.

"Yes ma'am. Unfortunately, Dominique is deceased ma'am. Our condolences..."

Mahalia wailed in the background almost obscuring the low humming that came from Ms. Robinson.

"Did she suffer?"

No one wanted to answer that question. Detective Moore looked to Phillips.

"No ma'am, she didn't."

She hummed again.

"Young man," Ms. Robinson turned in Phillips direction and looked right at him until he had no choice but to meet her gaze.

"Who are you trying to protect?"

Phillips fumbled, stuttered a bit; trying in his own way to save Ms. Robinson from the awful truth. Dr. Daniels could look at him and tell he was grappling for the right words to say, if there was such a thing. But Ms. Robinson would not be denied an answer.

"Now, I don't know how they do things where you from, but here, we tell folks the truth no matter how much it might hurt. You owe me the truth... I deserve the truth..."

Ms. Robinson's voice cracked but her gaze was unflinching. Phillips took a deep breath and momentarily dropped his gaze. She was unrelenting and eventually he lifted his head to face her again.

"Dominique was found on the side of the road. She was strangled to death."

Ms. Robinson gasped, covering her mouth with her hand. Phillips reached for the envelope sitting beside him and slowly pulled out the picture of Dominique lying on the steel gurney in the coroner's office. He handed the picture to Ms. Robinson. Positive identification was necessary for the criminal case. Ms. Robinson reluctantly accepted the picture. Before looking at the picture she looked toward heaven. The crease in her brow became drastically pronounced and the photo began to shake ever so slightly in her hand.

"Who did it? Who did that to my baby?"

"Unfortunately Ms. Robinson, we haven't found the perpetrator yet," Detective Phillips answered.

"You mean the devil that killed my Nique!"

"Yes ma'am."

"Mmmmmmmmmmmmmm...." Her face distorted again.

Ms. Robinson's brow furrowed deeply and she shook her head. Her body started to rock slowly as though instinctually consoling itself. Detective Moore, sitting closest to Ms. Robinson, extended her hand. Ms. Robinson quickly grabbed it with both hands squeezing it tight. It was her temporary anchor. She hummed again. It was heart-wrenching. Dr. Daniel's understood Ms. Robinson's grief reaction, considering the untenable nature of the situation.

Detective Phillips hung his head. Bearing witness to her sorrow pained him. No one dared interrupt her process.

Chloe Daniels took it all in, what was said and what wasn't. True to form, she observed her surroundings as much as she paid attention to Ms.

Robinson. The shotgun house was old but it was clean. The furnishings Ms. Robinson surrounded herself with were from another time. There was no modern gadgetry or useless trinkets to pollute her space. The music she enjoyed, she played on a record player; the albums stacked neatly inside the console.

"Ms. Robinson," Dr. Daniels asked, her voice low and consoling, "did Dominique have any tattoos?"

It took Ms. Robinson a moment to respond, and when she did, it was unexpected.

"Ha!"

A smile creased Ms. Robinson's face. Her eyes momentarily lit up.

"Yes! Nique defiled her body with that permanent ink. Boy did we go round and round about that."

Ms. Robinson laughed again.

"I never admitted to her that the one's she got wasn't that bad but it was the principal of the thing."

"Do you remember what they were?"

"Yes," Ms. Robinson answered. "Nique had a flower, I think a rose or something on her chest...she loved to wear her shirts just low enough to let that one show. She had another one that went all the way around her ankle. That one you only really saw in the summer time when she would wear shorts and stuff."

"The one on her ankle, what was that Ms. Robinson?" Phillips followed up.

"It was a link, almost like a chain with her name... Nique. That's what I always called her... mmmmmmm....." Her sorrow returned.

Pictures, presumably family pictures, hung in prominent positions on the walls. Generations of people were reflected there as evidenced by the black and white photos and antique framing. The plastic on the floral print living room furniture reminded Chloe of her grandmother. Every day visitors didn't sit in the living room in her grandmother's house. The kitchen is where family gathered. The living room was reserved especially for company. Ms. Robinson struck Chloe as much the same way.

Two pictures caught Dr. Daniel's eye; one was of Dominique and one was of a woman who Dominique favored more than she favored Ms. Robinson. The second woman was older and the pictures were hung close together.

"Ms. Robinson," Dr. Daniels began, "who is the woman in the picture?"

Ms. Robinson followed Dr. Daniels gaze and shook her head again.

"That's Nique's momma, my daughter, Karrie Ann..." Ms. Robinson's face saddened even more than it already was.

"Is she around?" Detective Phillips asked.

"Hmph... she hasn't been around for a while. That's why Nique lived with me... her and her momma both did for a while, but Karrie Ann ain't lived here in years."

"Do you have any way of getting in touch with her?" Phillips inquired.

"I wish I did, especially now... to know that her baby girl is gone.... Mmmm.... she so lost though..." A single tear fell from Ms. Robinson's eye.

"I hope you don't mind me asking, Ms. Robinson, but why did Karrie Ann leave?"

"She didn't leave, not on her own. I put her out! Chasing behind them no account men, one pipe dream after another... I made her leave Nique with me. I was tired of her traipsing that baby back and forth from here to yon', not knowing where they was gone end up. That wasn't no kind of life for a little girl. Karrie Ann was grown so if that's how she wanted to live that was fine with me but she wasn't gone be taking my grandbaby through it with her, no sir."

"When was the last time you saw Karrie Ann?"

"It's been a while, I would say a year or more. I stopped looking for her... long stopped praying she would get herself together. Karrie got mixed up with a fellow that got her strung out on that dope and turning tricks 'cause he was too lazy to get out and work himself. I tried to keep as much of that from Nique as I could... didn't want her to see her momma like that. She considered me her momma 'cause I raised her. But the older she got, she learned who her real momma was. That's kind of when all our problems started, when she learned the truth about Karrie Ann... made her question how her momma could leave her and not come see about her, care about her, you know? Karrie showing up out of nowhere hanging on some derelicts arm high out of her skull didn't help none either. I hated Nique had to see it. When you don't see a thing you can deny it. When you see it and your momma don't deny the wrong she's done to you, you can't deny it no more. "

"Is that when Dominique left for Atlanta?"

"Yes, but not right after. Nique stewed in that thing for a while; going over it and over it, asking me all kinds of questions I didn't have the answers for. She was angry, angry about her situation. Nique was really mad with her momma but she took it out on me. I understood that, didn't fault her for it. She was older and wanted to start experiencing things for herself. I can admit I kept a tight rein on her... didn't want her to end up like her momma. Maybe I held her too close to me but I was just trying to protect her. Nique didn't like that. She wanted to be grown and she felt like she couldn't do it here. So, she ventured out, snuck out one night...left me a note talking about moving to the big city to get her own life."

"Did she call while she was gone?" Detective Moore asked.

"Not when she first got there. I guess she was still real mad with me or having a good time, not sure. The last time I heard from Nique was about two weeks after she got to Atlanta. She called to tell me she was doing fine, having a good time and looking for work like she meant to stay there permanently. That was hard to hear, I missed her being around. But I didn't discourage her openly. I told her that I loved her and if she needed anything I was just a phone call away. That was the last time I talked to her." Ms. Robinson looked away from the group out towards the front of the house.

"She'll never come through that door again..."

"What ever happened to the last girl you hired?"

Drake asked over his morning coffee. It was Saturday morning and Drake was contending with a hangover. Parts of last night he didn't quite remember. What he did remember was his wife's flat out rejection of him. He had to soften her up, find a way to get back in her good graces. Taking time to converse with her to connect with her and put forth more effort was the only way he knew how.

Grace was immediately irked by his question as she scanned the computer looking at the referrals the agency sent over. She used her traditional service a couple of times but thought it best to change up her modus operandi; anything to avert suspicion.

"She didn't work out," Grace retorted, her words dripping with cynicism.

"Maybe I can help with the interviewing process, get more than one perspective."

"Do you think I am stupid Drake?"

"No, Gracie, why would you say that?"

"Let you help me with the interview, what, you want to pick out the next black bitch to sleep with?"

Drake almost gagged on his coffee. Regaining his composure, Drake offered a suggestion.

"You have got to get passed that Gracie," he began.

"Don't tell me what I have to get over and when..." Drake breezed by her comment not wanting to incite a riot.

"Tell you what, I'll help you with the interview and we'll pick someone who's not black."

Having him be a part of the process would totally throw a kink in her plan. Grace had to have a black girl... there were no if's, and's, or but's about that.

"I don't need your help, but thank you."

"You must. How many girls have you been through over the past three to four months? And none of them have worked out?"

Grace was steaming. How dare he question her process? Why did he care anyway? All he had to do was pay the bill. But with these girls there would be no bill so he should be satisfied.

"Fine! Fine! You want to dredge through interviewing the help then fine Drake. I will set the interviews for this afternoon."

Grace slammed the computer lid down and stormed away from the breakfast table. Drake continued to drink his coffee with a look of satisfaction on his face.

When his phone rang, Michael was barely conscious.

"Need you at the interchange Hwy 85," the voice on the other end of the phone commanded.

Hearing his boss on the other end forced Michael fully awake.

"Another body?"

"Yes, get on it."

The phone line disconnected before Michael had a chance to respond. He crawled out of bed, wiping the remaining remnants of sleep from his eyes. Hitting autodial, he placed the call.

"This can only mean one thing," Chloe said sleepily. Detective Phillips gave her the location.

"I'll meet you there." They had just parted ways a few hours earlier having traveled to and from South Carolina on the last notification. Crawling out of bed, Chloe stretched forcing herself to wake up. She padded down the hall and rapped on the guest room door.

"Duty calls," she whispered in to Addison who spent the night after combing through records and writing her report late into the midnight hour.

Traffic was at a near standstill. The combination of normal morning traffic, even on a Saturday and the slow cruisers trying to get a peek at the action on the side of the road made it sluggish going for Addison and Dr. Daniels to get to their destination. The scene Dr. Daniels and Addison arrived at was much like the last one. It was like déjà vu. Before their vehicle came to a complete stop, the media cameras and bright lights were already on them. The flashes otherwise diminished by the early morning sun magnified under the shadow cast by the overpass. The two climbed out of the vehicle and without responding to the onlookers or media personnel crossed the yellow dividing line. Peering out from his covered vantage point, he watched the whole thing in stilled silence.

There was no need for Dr. Daniels to consult with Phillips on what lie before them. The killer was the same; same m.o., same crude disposal, same mocking garbs and same clown-like makeup, but not quite the same. Dr. Daniels gloved up. Addison stood slightly behind.

"Take a look at this," Daniels gestured to Phillips.

Just as before the two crouched down over the body. They took a closer look at the victim's face. It was her eyes. There was something different about her eyes.

"That's not just make-up," Dr. Daniels said.

"No," Detective Phillips replied, "Those are injuries. Damn!"

Dr. Daniels looked back at Addison who was well ahead of her. She'd already made notes about the injury to the eyes highlighting the new development.

Dr. Daniels and Detective Phillips stood up and Phillips gave the nod for the body to be covered up.

"Get these people back!"

Phillips irritated disposition was clear as he forcefully moved toward the yellow tape and the crowd of media personnel encroaching upon the protected space. Several officers moved in, forcing the crowd back and then standing in front of the tape, blocking the view of the onlookers.

"She's only got one shoe," Addison said, pointing in the direction of the victim's feet. Both Daniels and Phillips who rejoined them took a closer look. The victim's other foot was loose in her shoe. With gloves on, Daniels lifted the shoe and examined it closely, finding common paper towels shoved into the toe.

"Where's her other shoe?"

Miriam was everything to the young Grace. She taught her what her mother couldn't; more importantly she taught Grace with unconditional love. For Grace, Miriam was more than just the help, she was her best friend. When Miriam left her without so much as a goodbye, little Grace was beyond consolable. Old Man Pembroke did his best to comfort his only child. He hired new nigger help and even bought Grace a puppy but neither replaced the love she had for Miriam. As a matter of fact, it embittered her more.

Young Grace's feelings were sometimes too big for her to put into words and so she didn't. She stopped talking. Her father didn't know what to make of it and the help found it difficult and cumbersome to try and communicate with her. She didn't give them a real chance, no matter how hard they tried to replace her Miriam. Things started happening that defied explanation. Mr. Pembroke's dinner would be burned; the stove turned on a much higher setting than the maid left it. Too much soap would be in the washer, causing it to overflow onto the black and white tiled floor. Little things, which if explainable, would be minor mishaps. But not in the Pembroke household. Old Man Pembroke would become infuriated. He was already low on tolerance and patience for the likes of the women he employed, so all it took was one such mistake before he found her replacement. Young Grace was always satisfied when the last one would leave, hoping the new one would really be the old one, her Miriam. When it didn't work out that way, Grace's antics would continue. She wouldn't be satisfied until she had her Miriam back.

Because of the high profile nature of the Anna Black case, the judicial decision was made by prosecutorial request to have Anna transferred outside of the city limits as she awaited trial. Having her in a more obscure, yet more secure correctional facility would dissuade the droves of people who gathered daily outside of the city-based jail, as well as potentially minimize the hordes of reporters looking to get the next story.

Traveling the 72 miles from downtown Atlanta to Alto Georgia, the home of Arrendale State Prison for women, took Addison and Chloe roughly an hour and a half. Once dense traffic was cleared in the downtown area, the highway was more open and the view more picturesque. Chloe used the time to review the files on Anna Black. Charged with multiple counts of murder in the first degree with premeditation, the prosecuting attorney, Geraldine Lassiter requested the court to appoint Dr. Daniels to conduct psychological assessments to determine Anna's fitness to stand trial. In essence, the courts, police, and anyone knowledgeable of the case, wanted to know if Anna Black was crazy. Chloe had her suspicions regarding Anna's mental state, but her personal musings mattered least of all. Her credibility as a forensic psychologist grew exponentially because her narration of the testing and open court testimony was infallible. No attorney to date had been able to get Dr. Daniels hung up on the details of differentiating her opinion from the evidence psychological examination offered. Chloe had every intention of keeping it that way.

Dr. Daniel's first encounter with Anna was unnerving. She fully expected this time to be no different. Addison had her own feelings about being exposed to Anna Black again. Against her better judgment, Addison decided to give voice to it before entering the prison.

"Where do you want me this time," Addison asked timidly.

Dr. Daniels heard the difference in her assistants' voice.

"What's going on?"

Addison took a second to figure out how she could put it. She didn't want to sound weak in front of her boss, but she also felt the need to let Dr. Daniels know the impact Anna Black had on her.

"Being on the other side of the glass was imposing," Addison began. "I just wanted to know how to prepare myself for this interview."

Dr. Daniels did her best to stifle a smile as she could see this was troubling her assistant.

"You do know she can't see through the two-way mirror, right?"

Addison knew that intellectually and fought back the natural tendency to pop her lips or roll her eyes at the suggestion. But this was Dr. Daniels, her mentor.

"Yes, I do know the mechanics of the two-way mirror," Addison began, doing her best not to sound trite. "But..."

"Go on," Dr. Daniels encouraged.

"Even though I know that, it felt like Anna was looking right at me."

Dr. Daniels stole a glance in her assistant's direction and saw that this was really bothering her. This was a teachable moment and Dr. Daniels wanted to treat it that way.

"Addison, you have great skill and tremendous insight. You will not always be an apprentice. At some point, you will be doing interviews on your own. Is Anna Black creepy? Absolutely! Sitting in there with her gave me the heebie jeebies!"

Both Addison and Chloe chuckled at her use of words.

"But I have a job to do, and so will you. It's rare that we like the clients we work with. They have committed heinous crimes and dealing with them up close and personal can make you sick to your stomach. But if we don't do it Addison, who will?"

Addison heard what her mentor had to say. She knew the importance of the work and Dr. Daniels' speech was a great reminder. Addison took a deep breath and nodded her head. She could do this, yeah, she could handle Anna Black.

Chloe and Addison, separately, steeled their emotions and braced themselves as Addison pulled the SUV up to the enormous concrete slab that currently served as Anna Black's residence. The sight was imposing; drab grayness on top of dull grayness, offset by the periodic glimmer of metallic shiny jagged-toothed barbed wire. There were windows, too small to clearly see out of and a see through, too tall fence to remind you of the perfunctory dividing line between freedom and incarceration. Chloe could feel the piercing, unwavering eyes of the guards as she and her assistant made their way across the rough graveled parking lot into the visitor's entrance. Chloe was grateful for that word, visitor.

The gated path leading to the entrance was tight, forcing the entrants to form a single-file line. The women on the yard closed in on those fenced in, making the space tighter and more claustrophobic even in open air. Addison and Dr. Daniels filed into the line uniformly, taking one small step and then another, keeping in time with the person immediately in front of them. There was little room to maneuver and no room for looking back. It was like the lead into a trap. Cat calls and cajoling pressed the visitors on both sides. The natural tendency was to look forward and not engage the prisoners, avoiding eye contact and focusing on taking the next step. Chloe buckled against that tendency, taking in the women who surrounded her; noting their sameness and their differences. The guard standing immediately near the entrance leveled an unwavering gaze upon the entrants. Nothing moved except her eyes, assessing everyone and everything, searching for disruption. Chloe could feel Addison's encroachment on her space. She was nervous, Chloe could tell because of her labored breathing.

Dr. Daniels passed through the doorway and into the holding area. Flashing her credentials she yielded to the customary search of her person and possessions. Addison was next, giving in to the unavoidable body check. Once they were cleared, the two were escorted by armed guard to the interview room. Steel rods, clanking keys and deadbolt locks isolated each path they took. The distinctively disturbing click of each lock echoed against lackluster walls, absent any signs of creativity. Arrendale was a women's prison guarded by women. That was intentional to dissuade sexual encounters between the caged and the watchers of the caged. Prisoners lived for those moments when fresh meat was around. It mattered not that Dr. Daniels and Addison were mere visitors. They were new, different; something the women hadn't seen in a while.

The guard opened the door to the room the interview would be held in. Once the women were inside, she promptly closed and locked the door behind them.

"Are you sure you want me in here?" Addison inquired; her angst and agitation showing. She would have much preferred to wait in the holding room or better yet in the car, but it was not to be, not this time.

"Yes, I want you here. I need your eyes and ears on this one."

Addison resigned herself to the inevitable and took the seat Chloe pointed her to. It was in the corner, away from the table where Dr. Daniels and soon Anna Black would be sitting. Addison's role in the doctor's practice had increased since they first began working together. Addison knew she was more than an assistant and she appreciated the doctor having so much confidence in her abilities. Addison was herself well versed in forensic psychology, having completed her doctoral studies and working on her dissertation. But being in the room with a known killer was disconcerting for Addison. She'd read everything Dr. Daniels had available on Anna Black. Although intrigued, Addison couldn't wait for this part of her job to be over.

Dr. Daniels readied herself for the interview. She always found serial killers to be most fascinating. There was something about how their minds worked, the rationalizations they so easily made, what prompted them to become judge and juror, exacting the kill... Chloe mused her fascination may be part of the reason she remained single, although eligible. Most people were unnerved by the things she delved into wholeheartedly. What man wanted to discuss murder over dinner? Not many and not one she found. There was one who piqued her interest but he'd been hesitant and clumsy in his approach.

Hearing the undeniable sound of the guards' keys processing the lock drew Chloe back to the situation at hand. She took a deep breath and waited for her client to enter.

Dr. Daniels saw the guard extend her arm to hold the door open before she saw Anna. The prisoners' head was down. A mass of unkempt dirty platinum blonde hair with darkened roots covered Anna's face. She shuffled in; both her arms and ankles bound with heavy chain and cuffs that stifled her movement. The orange uniform of the imprisoned fell loosely from Anna's slight frame. There was a second guard following closely behind her. Once Anna was fully in the room, the guard pulled the chair back. The guard who accompanied Anna into the room bypassed the one still standing at the door. The remaining guard looked to Dr. Daniels and advised they'd be standing right outside the door. Addison was relieved to hear it and Dr. Daniels nodded her understanding.

The door closed securely and the humming started. It was Anna's signature song. "Hush little baby, don't say a word..." This time Dr. Daniels wasn't surprised. Anna didn't raise her head until she'd sat down and finished humming the chorus of her song. When she did look up Anna smiled. Splintery shivers coursed down Addison's back. Anna's smile defied her face. It was as if a puppet master maneuvered his fingers and strings attached to the edges of her thin lips turned up on queue. The rest of her face was sunken and sallow but her eyes, Anna's eyes were dark; not in color but in intensity. They didn't smile with her mouth.

"Good afternoon Anna," Dr. Daniels began. "I hope you don't mind but I have my assistant with me today." Chloe gestured in Addison's direction. Addison didn't quite know how to respond. Should she wave, speak, smile? Just as Addison prepared to respond to the acknowledgement, Anna turned her focus directly to the corner where Addison sat. The luminescent glow from the overhead lights cast a disquieting shadow over Addison, but she felt Anna's gaze piercing through it, finding her unprepared.

"I don't mind at all, Dr. Daniels," Anna quipped. "Don't mind at all..." She continued to stare through Addison making the assistant adjust uncomfortably in her chair.

"Anna," Dr. Daniels said, attempting to draw her attention back, "I need to ask you a series of questions. I want you to answer them as honestly as possible. Understand?"

There was silence. Anna appeared besotted with Addison, unable or unwilling to drop her piercing gaze.

"Anna?"

Dr. Daniels started to second guess her decision to have her assistant present, but Anna's actions confirmed some of her earlier inclinations regarding Anna's personality type. The room fell awkwardly silent with the exception of clanking from Anna's confinement chains. Her hands were underneath the table so Dr. Daniels had no idea what she was doing to cause the links to sound off. Cautiously she observed Anna.

"I'm ready for the questions doctor," Anna replied after another extended pause. There was some relief there for Dr. Daniels. Part of the psychological evaluation was determining if the person was oriented to the present; able to attend to the things that were immediately taking place. Although physically Anna presented as disengaged, at some level mentally, she was attending.

"Okay, let's get started. Anna do you know what day is it?"

"Tuesday." Her eyes never left the corner of the room.

"What year is it?"

"It is the year two thousand and sixteen. It's been that for six months now. Next question."

"Who is the current president?" Dr. Daniels inquired, establishing the necessary baseline for further inquiry.

"President Barack Hussein Obama," Anna replied confidently. Dr. Daniels noted the confidence. Addison, taking notes from the interview, refused to look up. She felt the penetration of Anna's stare.

"Anna, for the next part of our time together, I am going to make some statements. I want you to answer true or false. If there is more that you would like to add, then please feel free to do so."

Anna verbalized no response.

"Ready?"

"Sure doctor."

"First statement: I can be very smooth, engaging, charming, slick. True or false?"

For the first time since she sat down, Anna turned her eyes towards Dr. Daniels. There was no smile there. The brash sound of chains moving sounded again.

"Smooth, slick, what does that mean doctor?" Anna's affect was as flat as her intonations. The attempt to cover the irritation from the questions was lackluster at best.

"It doesn't matter what it means to me, Anna, what do the words mean to you?"

The prisoner didn't blink. Was she pondering, thinking, contemplating a witty rhetorical comeback? Dr. Daniels wasn't sure. She had no doubt Anna had the capacity for it, though.

"Well doctor, the way you are putting it, smooth sounds like a bad thing and slick certainly does."

Giggling, Anna covered her mouth with her chained hand. Her laughter was nearly as unsettling as her smile.

"To answer your question, doctor, I am engaging but not slick. I can be charming but not smooth."

"Would you say true or false, Anna?"

"I would say what I said."

"Okay, next statement, true or false: I can give a very self-conscious and confident impression, and it is hard to make me speechless; I can talk someone into the ground if needed."

"That's more than one statement."

Anna had removed her hands from her face and sat them down on the table. She started drumming her fingers. Her actions were duly noted.

"I can give a very self-conscious and confident impression. True or false?"

"That's much better, true," Anna replied, her eyes still dark. Yet, a victorious smile played around her lips.

"It is hard to make me speechless. True or false?"

"I would have to say true... especially today... your assistant made me speechless... such a child-like quality to her... innocent... needy..."

Anna didn't look in Addison's direction. She didn't need to. She knew how weighty her words were. Addison was startled by the commentary, yet, she understood how important it was to not react. Instead, Addison kept focused on her notes, despite the creepy crawling sensation accosting her skin. Dr. Daniels attempted to minimize the meandering and proceeded with the next statement.

"I can talk someone into the ground if needed."

"That's a ridiculous statement. False."

Dr. Daniels pressed forward.

"Next, true or false. I can be very self-assured, opinionated, even a braggart."

"Self-confidence is important and so is having an opinion. You don't want to look like an idiot. True," Anna responded, completely disregarding the third component of the statement.

"Sometimes I might have an inflated view of my abilities and be cocky."

"I like this question, doctor. Out of all the questions you've asked me so far, this one I like. The answer is false. I don't have an inflated view of my abilities. I know exactly what I am capable of... helping people... easing their pain... relieving their sorry pitiful lives... saving them from themselves and the other stupid people in their lives."

"What people have you helped Anna?"

The question wasn't a part of the DSM-IV standardized statements but Dr. Daniels wanted to evaluate her responsiveness.

There was no hesitancy in Anna's willingness to entertain the doctors' inquiry. The smile returned, just as unnerving as it had been the first time.

"Is that a trick question doctor?" Anna elongated doctor in a sing-songy way, worthy of the appearance of goose bumps to the flesh.

"No Anna, it's not."

"Then why ask? You already know the people I've helped…"

"Are there some I don't know about?"

Addison's ears perked up. She had avoided making eye contact with Anna as much as humanly possible but she wanted to see what Anna would say to this question, how she would respond.

The smile never faded; yet, Anna's hooded eyes reflected her annoyance with Dr. Daniel's persistence.

"Do you think I'm stupid?"

Increased tinkling from the chains signaled a shift in the atmosphere. Anna didn't wait for the doctor to respond when she asked the question again.

"Do you think I'm stupid doctor?!?"

Anna was animated, more than she'd ever been before. The anger that had been cloistered behind her smile spilled out like hot liquid. Without further provocation, Anna slammed her chained hands on the table. The sound echoed, bouncing off the dully painted walls and ringing in the ears of its occupants. Dr. Daniels didn't respond verbally or physically but Addison nearly jumped out of her skin. The solace of having the two guards outside the room, one watching from the one way mirror, kept Chloe from recoiling. She put up her hand, signaling to the watchers that everything was okay and not to enter the room. From the increased rise and fall of Anna's shoulders, one could sense she was fuming. Her skin transitioned from pale to flushed pink. Dr. Daniels fully expected that after a few moments Anna would calm down and return to her coy self, but that was not to be, not today. She started to rock, slowly at first, back and forth and back and forth again, faster with more intent. Self-soothing maybe? Dr. Daniels was not sure.

Low animalistic sounds began to emanate from Anna's mouth. The rocking continued and the utterances kept pace with each rocking motion. To ask another question or attempt to break through Anna's trance-like state may prove difficult but Dr. Daniels needed to see the full manifestation of the inmate's psychosis.

"Anna, is there something you'd like to share?"

Dr. Daniels' sentiments could well be seen as mordacious. She was willing to take the risk.

Anna's limp hair moved swiftly in the wind she created. Steely eyes glared at Dr. Daniels and she returned the intense gaze; asserting herself as one not afraid of Anna's wrath. It was a showdown of wills and neither of the two refused to buckle. Addison looked from one woman to the other. The tension in the room was suffocating. Then she moved. Shoving the table and simultaneously rising to her feet, all the rage Anna could spare was unleashed. Dr. Daniels pushed back but not in enough time to avoid the hard edge of the table slamming into her midsection. Addison stood to her feet dropping everything on her lap and moved in the direction of her boss.

Anna couldn't find the words or maybe she didn't. She growled, low and guttural crescendoing to a high pitched deafening squeal. Before Anna could move any further, the interview room door swung open and both guards pounced. Anna refused to be contained any further than the chains that physically bound her. She fought violently against the guards, thrashing and wriggling to keep away from their grasps. The guards refused to be defeated and quickly gained control of her, slamming her into the table still sitting catawampus in the middle of the room. Anna groaned and exhaled loudly as if all the wind in her frail body had been forcefully compressed.

Then she cackled; a complete audio assault on the ears.

"Is this what you wanted doctorrrrrrrrr?"

"Let's move Black," the guard insisted before Dr. Daniels had a chance to respond.

"HUSH LITTLE BABY DON'T SAY A WORD, MOMMA'S GONNA BUY YOU A FUCKIN' MOCKINGBIRD!"

Anna's song continued long down the hallway.

"Tell me what you thought about the interview?" Dr. Daniels asked Addison as they made their way back to the city.

Chloe's assistant still looked visibly shaken. Addison could still feel the cold dead eyes of Anna Black boring through her, piercing to reach her soul. She could still hear that shrill laugh. How could she demonize a baby's lullaby? Addison thought to herself as she continued to navigate the highway; her supervisor's question rolling around in her head. The whole thing gave Addison the creeps but she had to present as strong and professional to Dr. Daniels. She would love to tell Chloe, the part of her boss she considered her friend, exactly what she thought, but Addison wanted to impress Dr. Daniels.

"I think a lot can be gleaned from meeting with Ms. Black. Certainly, she meets several of the criteria outlined by the DSM IV-R for narcissistic personality disorder and dare I say sociopathic tendencies." Addison pushed up her glasses resting them securely on the bridge of her nose. Chloe observed her assistant, her student, and smiled. Then she snickered which caught Addison completely off guard.

"Was there something wrong with my tentative diagnosis?" Addison looked to Dr. Daniels and then quickly back to the road.

"No, no, your assessment was fine," Chloe continued. "But I really want to know what you think, you Addison, not the scholarly you."

Addison contemplated what Dr. Daniels said and stole another look in her direction. Seeing the smile still dancing on her supervisor's lips she lightened up.

"Okay, because that was one of the freakiest, creepiest situations I have ever been in," Addison replied, her shoulders relaxing for the first time since they'd left the prison.

"I mean, she's crazy, not just diagnostically crazy but really crazy..."

Chloe laughed along with Addison; tickled by Addison's uncharacteristic animation.

"I probably shouldn't call her crazy," Addison recoiled apologetically.

"No, I understand, truly I do."

"How do you deal with it?" Addison inquired sincerely, the light moment having passed.

"It was hard at first," Chloe reflected. "I used to take things personally and not be able to separate work from non-work. That stuff gets better with time. You learn to compartmentalize... that's how you stay sane when dealing with crazy folks."

The two shared another brief round of laughter. Addison didn't miss what Dr. Daniels had to say about keeping things separate. If she was to successfully follow in her mentors' footsteps she would certainly have to master that one.

"Once we get back to the house, I want you to transcribe the recording so I can start the process of pulling this stuff together for court. They are going to want my recommendations sooner than later. Trying to get through another interview with Anna may be difficult but necessary if I don't have enough to work with."

Addison could tell they were drawing closer to the city limits as traffic started to drag. Dr. Daniels was quiet for the remainder of the ride, reviewing in her mind the exchange she'd just had with Anna and thinking about the three women that were still unidentified.

Chapter Ten

Grace's frustration with her husband did not diminish as she scoured the internet in search of a nanny service she hadn't used before. She was convinced of his motives for wanting to be involved in the interviewing process. When Drake walked into the office on her as she searched, Grace almost blew a gasket.

Drake sat down behind his wife and began to browse over her shoulder.

"What about her," he inquired, his breath wreaking of too much distilled liquor. Grace wrinkled her nose and tried to ignore his comment.

"Get a mint or something. Better yet, go brush your teeth. Your breath is horrid," Grace complained.

"I'm just trying to help Gracie. Obviously, you need it. Either your selection process needs work or maybe your people skills."

Drake didn't jab back too frequently but when he did, he was smart about it; never overtly fighting, never brawling, just quiet, calm, retaliation.

"You make me so sick," Grace seethed. Drake dismissed it.

"I'll be back in a moment after I freshen up. Don't set up any interviews until I return," Drake replied matter of factly.

"Tuh," Grace scoffed.

She turned her attention back to the computer screen, grabbed hand sanitizer from the corner of the desk, and voraciously cleaned her hands. She wanted to replace the smell of stale bourbon in the room with the much more aromatic scents of lavender and antiseptic. Grace hated when Drake exercised the authority he knew he possessed and she had no choice but to eventually honor because he was, in fact, the only breadwinner. Grace couldn't afford to be frozen out of the finances. Old man Pembroke didn't leave her with a tremendous inheritance so Grace understood the need to play the game, if only for the money.

Drake returned a few minutes later with a fresh shirt on. When he sat down slightly behind Grace, she could smell the overpowering scent of mouthwash lingering on his breath. At least it was better than smelling like a distillery, Grace thought to herself.

"Are you ready," she asked coldly.

"Of course, dear."

She hated when he was syrupy sweet to her. Grace knew he didn't mean it. Grace located a site she hadn't used before and the two began to go through the profiles. Those that didn't have a picture, Grace immediately skipped over. She needed to know exactly what the help would look like before scheduling an interview.

"What about her," Drake inquired, sounding hopeful. The one he pointed out was Hispanic.

"No, she won't do," Grace clipped.

"Why? She seems perfectly qualified. Did you look at her resume?"

"She won't do."

Grace quickly clicked the computer mouse and moved to another group of potentials.

Drake did his best not to get frustrated but his wife was truly testing his patience.

Grace clicked through quickly until she found a page with Black women on it. He may have done it subconsciously but Drake leaned in a little closer. Grace was repulsed but kept her cool. The girl she would select would be for her, not him. She needed a new girl. The desire to kill grew with each successful one.

"She's perfect," Grace said, more for herself than for him.

"Which one," Drake asked, leaning in so far now his chest was pressed against Grace's back.

Grace pointed on the screen. Madeline St. James was the help Grace chose. Drake disregarded her qualifications and looked at her. She was stunning; chocolaty skin, a mess of curly hair, full lips. He resisted the urge to lick his own lips. He memorized her face. Madeline would be his inspiration for the night. Drake was mindful not to linger too long staring at the screen. He leaned back, creating greater distance between himself and the one he married.

"We should at least interview her," he replied nonchalantly. "But shouldn't we select at least one more, just in case?"

Grace thought about it for a moment. When she hired Madeline, and she intended to hire Madeline, she could have another one waiting in the wings. Then she wouldn't have to go through the hassle of finding another girl and Drake wanting to be involved. The only concern had was both girls were from the same service. That could make things tricky.

"I guess it wouldn't hurt," Grace conceded.

The two perused the site some more, finding nothing that satisfied them. What was offered just wasn't measuring up.

"She might do," Grace suggested of a Black woman with fair skin and short cropped hair. She waited to see what her husband's response would be. It was like a game of cat and mouse. If he responded with too high a level of excitement, Drake was convinced Grace would bypass the woman for someone he was less responsive too. If he didn't show any interest, Drake knew that would be the one she'd select, just to spite him. Even though he intended to never sleep with the help again, Drake appreciated having something yummy to look at. This second girl, she wasn't necessarily his preference, but she was still pretty... still better looking than his pasty wife.

"Set it up. The sooner the better."

"Are you available this afternoon," Grace called after him as Drake exited the office.

"Yes."

His response was flat but sufficient. Grace immediately got on the phone to the agency and arranged the interviews. She would set them 30 minutes apart. The St. James girl would be first. Grace knew her husband would lend his support to her. She would keep the second girl, Carmen Moore, as a replacement for the soon to be deceased Madeline. The agency was able to accommodate the interviews for the afternoon and Grace was pleased about that. The faster the preliminary processes were over, the sooner she could get on to the most important phase.

He overheard their conversation from his perch underneath the overpass. He paid close attention to the detective and the lady bending over the body. He heard them make a comment about a missing shoe; a shoe he now had in his possession. It was in his shopping cart where he kept those things most important to him; the one he kept hidden behind a board and old fencing that was discarded. He watched everything and waited... waited to see if the killer would visit again...

Madeline St. James arrived promptly at 2:30 p.m. Grace intentionally set the appointment to overlap with her children getting in from school. Grace did this more to sell the ruse than anything so Drake could gauge how well she interacted with the children, thereby bolstering Grace's already decided position that Madeline should be the choice. Drake was excited that there would be another woman in the house, if only for a little while. He knew the necessity of maintaining professional couth so as not to raise suspicion with his wife. But after seeing Madeline's picture on the web, he couldn't wait to see her in person. She already made his night, virtually. Seeing Madeline in the flesh would aid in his visual fantasy, when he knew he would stroke his self in her honor.

When Madeline entered the home, she had a cool confidence that was somewhat off-putting for Grace. She fully expected the help to be groveling, sniveling and vying to get the penny Anny job for whatever scrap of wages she would offer. Everyone knew, the only thing Blacks were good for was doing the grunt work, like the Mexicans. So when Madeline St. James came in and didn't lower her eyes when she was introduced and didn't show all her teeth in a goofy buffoon grin, Grace instantly wanted to bring her down to size. But she knew she couldn't be quite as cool and callous as she normally was. Drake was watching. Besides, she needed a fresh offering to feed her murderous intentions. So Grace played nice, not too nice, but just nice enough.

Drake appreciated Madeline even more in person. The picture of her on the internet really didn't do her good looks justice. He paid close attention to the smoothness of her café Olay skin tone, the fullness of her pouty lips and the deepness of her dark eyes. When Grace wasn't looking, he allowed his gaze to follow her figure. Underneath her neat white blouse and black dress slacks, Drake could see her curves; slight but distinct. His manhood responded as his eyes memorized every facet of the woman who stood before him.

After the trio was seated at the kitchen table, Grace began the interview process.

"So Maude, do you have any experience as a housekeeper?"

"Madeline, ma'am, my name is Madeline, and although I am capable of housekeeping, my focus is providing childcare services."

How dare this trollop correct me, Grace thought to herself as she pursed her lips, ready to chastise the harlot for her clear overstatement. However, Drake interjected, taking the sting out of what she was about to say.

"A focus on childcare, would you care to elaborate Ms. St. James?"

"Madeline is fine, Mr. Wetherby," the potential help began. "I am currently studying child development at Georgia State University and having an opportunity to be a nanny will give me a chance to utilize what I've learned."

Grace didn't like how confidently the girl spoke. She clearly needed to be taken down a notch or two.

"So, you want to practice on our children?"

Grace's comment was cool and snide. Drake shot her a look that shouted how out of line her remark was.

"I don't think practice is the word for it, dear," Drake interjected.

"No, I wouldn't say practice," Madeline explained. "Because of my studies, I can relate the children's behavior to the stage of development they are in and ensure my interaction with them fosters age appropriate actions."

High falooting bitch, Grace thought but didn't say. Her face showed her disapproval. Grace was moving in the wrong direction. She needed this girl more than anyone so she plastered on a smile that was a fragile as fine china and tried to shift the conversation before the girl lost interest.

"That sounds fine, since you have the education," Grace began. It was disingenuous and Madeline began to pull away and disengage. Drake noticed the young lady lean back and rest her back against the chair. He needed to reel her back in.

"If you do decide to accept the position, accommodations can be a part of your compensation. Hopefully that would help to defray any housing costs and the cost of traveling back and forth. Bus service doesn't exactly come to the house so if you don't have your own vehicle, I'm sure we can make additional accommodations if necessary." Drake did his best to make the job sound appealing.

Just then the door opened. Preston and Mary Lou came barreling through the door.

"Dad," Mary Lou exclaimed. "I'm surprised you're here!"

"Hey there Punkin'," Drake said, hugging Mary Lou back who had already grabbed him around the neck. "Just helping mommy find a new nanny."

"What happened to the last one," Preston asked, plopping down in the seat between Madeline and his dad. "I kinda liked her." Preston was nearly pouting and Grace didn't appreciate it. She was still their mother and no matter of house help could take her place. But she didn't respond to her ungrateful son. Instead she refocused everyone's attention on the girl who sat before them.

"Preston, Mary Lou, say hi to Ma-de- line, is it?"

Madeline nodded her head, refusing to respond to the rudeness of the woman interviewing her. She had to stay focused on what was most important and landing this job would be just what she needed to bolster her resume. Madeline only had one semester left before graduation. Having practical experience would set her apart as she applied for an advanced degree. So Madeline didn't respond to the snide comments or the harsh looks from the Mrs. She kept focused on the bigger picture.

Mary Lou was the first to respond.

"Hi Ms. Madeline, it's nice to meet you," the little girl beamed.

"It's very nice to meet you too, Mary Lou. I like your pretty dress," Madeline replied.

"Thank you," Mary Lou said.

"I like her daddy, she's nice," the youngster whispered in her father's ear loud enough for everyone at the table to hear. Grace resisted the urge to roll her eyes in the top of her head. The cheap compliment on her daughter's attire didn't impress her.

"She is nice," Drake responded, smiling in Madeline's direction and then quickly straightening his face as Grace cut her eyes in his direction.

"Preston offered a hello as well; not quite as exuberantly as Mary Lou, but it was pleasant nonetheless.

"Nice to meet you as well Preston. Did you have a good day at school," Madeline inquired.

Preston nodded his head and fiddled with his backpack.

"Alright children, put your school things away and head upstairs to start your homework," Grace commanded, regaining control of the conversation.

"Do we have to," Mary Lou whimpered.

"Of course you do, dear," Grace corrected.

"Do what mommy said," Drake advised and gave his daughter a kiss to the forehead, shooing her on her way. Preston dragged himself from the table and then dragged his backpack on the floor behind him.

Grace was incensed. Before she could demand Preston pick it up, Madeline backed her chair from the table and walked over to Preston as he exited the kitchen.

"Let me help you with that," Madeline said, picking up the pack and helping Preston put it back on.

"Thank you Ms. Madeline," Preston replied, offering her the first smile since he'd been home. Grace scoffed. Preston put some pep in his step and bounded up the stairs behind his sister. Madeline made her way back to the table. Grace didn't like the fact her children addressed the help as miss. A salutation of that kind was reserved for a person deserving of acknowledgment. It represented deference she was sure the young girl didn't deserve. It was a good thing this one wouldn't be around very long. Grace would make sure her children wouldn't address the next one that way.

Once the children were out of the room and Madeline returned to her seat, Grace commenced to wrapping up the interview. The girl had been in her house long enough and Drake was barely able to keep himself from drooling. Grace just needed to get the final details so she could start working on her own plan for this one's demise.

"If we were to offer you the job, how would you get here," Grace asked with her pen poised over her notepad.

"For now public transportation," Madeline replied.

"If she takes the job, I'm sure we can help with that."

Grace didn't bother acknowledging his comment. He was lusting. Of that Grace was sure. His tongue was damn near wagging from his pathetic mouth.

"And when can you start?"

Drake found his eyes and his mind wandering. He really couldn't help it. The last time he had decent sex was with the nanny that was fired. Grace had never really been a decent lay. She was available, that was it. There was no excitement, just husbandly duty to a less than enticing wife. Drake crossed his legs to hide his masculine reaction. He might not be able to wait until tonight to handle himself.

"If we can agree to the pay, I can start tomorrow," Madeline replied.

The fact that needing to 'agree to the pay' was even a conversation she insisted on having peeved Grace. But she had to remind herself, the bitch wouldn't have the chance to cash in, let alone earn the first payment. Grace didn't overtly protest, allowing Drake to handle that portion of the conversation. Grace crossed her bony arms over her tiny breasts and watched the interaction between the two. Was Madeline being too friendly with her husband? Smiling and maintaining unwavering eye contact... Clearly, this one thought she was higher than her allotted station but Grace would take her down more than a peg. She would put the bitch in her rightful place.

As Madeline exited the eloquent home, she was very pleased with herself. Not only did she land the job, but she also smartly negotiated a higher salary over their initial offer. Madeline was no fool, though. She knew the Mrs. would be a problem, but she already had the man of the house eating out of her hand.

Chapter Eleven

Drake waited until he knew the children were down for the night before retiring to his own bedroom. He didn't want Grace to have the excuse of the children, on top of all the other bullshit excuses she made for not fulfilling her responsibilities to him as her husband. Tonight, Drake wouldn't take no for an answer. He downed the last drops of black label bourbon he had in his snifter and shakily made his way up the stairs to the master bedroom. Grace was already in bed. When her delinquent husband entered, she pulled the duvet up near her ears and tucked it under her legs. Drake stumbled clumsily through the bedroom, nearly knocking over a standing lamp before disrobing down to his briefs and plunking down onto the bed.

The fact that he didn't bother to go into the bathroom to freshen up disgusted Grace even more. She could smell the liquor wafting from his person. She pulled the cover up over her nose to try and quell the stench. Drake wasn't sober enough to be concerned about her feelings. He needed some ass and his wife was going to give it to him, plain and simple. Drake pressed his skivvies up against her thick cotton gown so she could feel his manhood growing. His thoughts were of another but that didn't matter to Drake. He needed a vessel. He could close his eyes and dismiss the package.

Grace wriggled away from him, scooting as close to the edge of the bed as she could without falling off. Her deep sighs of disgust were wasted on the determined Drake. He moved to her, closing the distance. He burrowed under the covers and roughly threw his arm around her waist to keep her from escaping. Realizing she had no place to go, Grace braced for what she knew would come next.

She felt his sloppy lips on her neck as he nuzzled her hair with his nose.

"Drake, please stop," Grace spat; in no way attempting to hide her disdain.

He dismissed her. She didn't really mean it. Drake continued to pursue Grace wriggling his hand harshly into her lackluster panties. Drake gripped her flat ass, steadily pushing his growing penis against her. Grace squirmed but he held her tight. When Drake heavy-handedly groped her vagina, Grace tensed up, but her body defied her resolve. Drake found wetness between her thin thighs and moaned deeply, convinced he was pleasing her.

Drake was beyond restraint as he threw the duvet off himself and as much off his wife as was possible. Getting up on his knees, Drake grabbed Grace turning her over. She resisted, but even drunk on his ass, Drake was too powerful. Grace found herself face to face with a man she detested. Their eyes connected and she could see lust, not love, but pure uncontained lust. Grace knew that look wasn't for her.

Drake leaned in as he pushed himself between her clenched legs and pushed out his lips as if to kiss her. Grace was sickened by his audacity. Wriggling her arm free, Grace slapped Drake's face as hard as she could. Drake recoiled; his face beet red. Grace took the opportunity to push her teetering fool of a husband back, just enough to get from under him.

"You frigid bitch," Drake seethed, no longer fighting to stay on top of her, but going with her attempt at pushing him off. He rolled onto his side of the bed as Grace recovered herself, putting emphasis on tucking the duvet around herself.

"Fuck you, you ingrate," Grace shot back, turning and looking over her shoulder to make sure Drake heard her. The room grew quiet as the two stewed in their own frustration.

And then Grace's ears perked up as she heard disquieting sounds from her husbands' side of the bed. At first, Grace couldn't discern the cause of the noise but soon it became clear. The repeated sloshing and slapping sound and the occasional grunt from her inebriated spouse solidified the horrible visual image in her head. He was fantasizing and jacking himself off. Grace knew his fantasies were of the girl; that low life black piece of trash she allowed in her home. So common, Grace thought as she pulled the overworked duvet cover over her ear to help drown out the repugnant sound.

The rhythmic slapping sounds continued and Drake's moans and groans grew louder. Grace had been instrumental in replacing one fantasy for another with the introduction of the newest help. She was sickened by the thought. Grace closed her eyes and did her best to tune out Drake's nauseating display. A dark smile found its way across Grace's lips as she too began to engage in her own fantasies about Mad-e-line…

The phone for Dr. Daniels seemed to be ringing off the hook. No sooner did Addison end one call did the busy phone ring again. Dr. Daniels couldn't be bothered to answer it or take any calls at the moment. She was knee-deep in diagnostic material and a review of her most recent interview with the now infamous Anna Black.

"Dr. Chloe Daniels office, how may I help you," Addison replied to the next phone call; balancing the phone on her shoulder and a pad and pen in her hands.

Addison listened intently as the caller provided the information. When she disconnected, she politely interrupted Dr. Daniels who was sitting behind her cluttered desk.

"That was the prosecutor's office," Addison began once she secured Chloe's undivided attention.

Looking up from the mounds on her desk, Chloe sighed deeply. Whatever it was, she knew it couldn't be good; not this close to the trial.

"What is it," Chloe said flatly, lacing her fingers behind her head, and sitting back in her Italian leather work chair.

"There has been an unexpected change in prosecutorial personnel," Addison mimicked, much to Chloe's delight. Addison knew of the often contentious relationship between Dr. Daniels and the county prosecutors' office so making fun of them was always welcomed.

"Who?" Dr. Daniels asked, leaning forward and putting her elbows on her desk.

"Judith M. Norwood Esquire, will be the new representative from their office."

"Mmhmm, and will this delay the trial?" Chloe asked. Considering how things transpired with the last Anna Black interview, a delay could work to her benefit.

"Of course they promised that this change in personnel would in no way delay justice," Addison replied.

Chloe let herself fall back in her chair. Her hands were steepled and her thumbs were twirling. Addison knew that posture. She could see her boss's wheels turning.

"What are you thinking," Addison inquired.

It took Dr. Daniels a minute before replying.

"A delay on the prosecutor's part would have been great," Dr. Daniels began. "I have poured over all the information on Anna. Although I feel like we have something to work with here, doing one more interview may be necessary. Not to mention, I haven't even begun to formulate a diagnostic hypothesis on this new killer."

Dr. Daniels paused again as she contemplated the situation.

"Procedurally, though, I could propose a delay because of the change in personnel... hmmm... needing to bring them up to speed, reviewing my testimony...you know Judith can be beastly..."

Addison was well aware of Ms. Norwood's reputation. Judith Norwood was a woman on a mission to get to the top of the food chain and she didn't care who she had to use, step on or step over to get there.

"But my proposition of a delay could somehow suggest I am the reason for the delay. That wouldn't bode well for the office."

Addison nodded her head, understanding the predicament Chloe could find herself in. "Let me think about it for a minute."

Addison dutifully scribbled some reminder notes into her trusty notebook.

"I wonder if Michael knows about the change."

Addison's eyebrow raised slightly. Rarely if ever did Dr. Daniels refer to Detective Phillips by his first name. Addison smiled as she busied herself with her own stack of documents to review. She knew the last statement was rhetorical and not meant for an audible response from her.

Dr. Daniels excused herself from the room and took the phone with her. She hit speed dial as she made her way to the master bedroom.

The recipient picked up on the first ring.

"Detective Phillips," Chloe addressed him as she lay casually across her neatly made bed.

Michael was pleasantly surprised by her call. Even though Chloe addressed him formally, there was something in her voice that seemed more personal. Maybe it was just wishful thinking on his part. Nevertheless, Michael was glad to hear from her.

"Dr. Daniels," he replied, equally as formal yet he was smiling.

Chloe heard the way in which he addressed her and knew he was being funny.

"I hope I'm not disturbing you," she began.

"Not at all. What can I help you with?"

Michael was doing his best to remain the consummate professional but there was a soothing sound to Chloe's voice that did something to him, even when she was keeping it straight. Maybe it came from her years in private practice counseling people and assuaging their problems away.

"Well, I was just wondering if you'd heard about the change of prosecutor."

"This close to the beginning of trial? Is this going to set us back? I mean, with this other situation popping off, delaying Black's trial could make for significant backlash."

Chloe smiled as his questions and commentary overlapped. He said everything she was thinking. It was good to see their ideas about the matter were simpatico. The backlash would be epic, not only for the police department but quite possibly for her office. Michael continued to vent his frustrations. She waited until he finished and offered what answers she had.

"No delay? We'll see about that," Michael scoffed. Chloe knew the detective's relationship with the prosecutor's office was just about as cantankerous as hers. On that the two certainly agreed.

"We will definitely see," Chloe concurred. "Any new developments with the second serial killer," Chloe asked, briefly changing the subject.

"The baby doll killer?"

"Ugh, I hate that name," Chloe cringed.

"It is pretty bad," Michael laughed.

It was good to hear him laugh, Chloe thought. She had an idea of the level of stress Michael was under, so any opportunity to find humor was a good one. Chloe found herself chuckling with him. After the laughter died down, Michael replied.

"It's actually been about a week since the last kill. I would have expected the time between murders to shorten, unless..."

"Unless?"

"Unless the killer has stopped," Michael offered.

But just like Dr. Daniels, he knew the likelihood of that was slim to none. That kind of behavior would suggest something happened to the killer that prevented them from being able to commit additional crimes. It was a possibility but with low probability. Most serial killers couldn't stop and the time between deaths typically decreased. Unless the baby doll killer was out of commission, there would be another victim.

"I expect another body soon," Michael thought aloud.

"We need a break in this case," Chloe answered.

"Maybe we'll get something in the morning."

"I certainly hope so."

Dr. Daniels and Addison met Detective Phillips at the coroner's office early the next day. They must have arrived earlier than Dr. Wakefield Brookes expected. He was finishing his hearty breakfast of runny eggs, grits and toast very near to the covered body. Addison turned up her nose at the thought of food consumption with a dead body within inches. As the three approached, Dr. Brookes wiped the remains of breakfast from his lips and stood up.

"Morning folks," Dr. Brookes said, still chewing.

"Morning doc," Detective Phillips replied.

The four gathered around the body and Dr. Brookes pulled back the white sheet. Addison turned on the recorder to capture the findings.

"I wish I could tell you the killer got careless and left us more with this one than the others, but whoever it is, they are very careful."

"There are two differences that are worth noting," Dr. Brookes continued, pointing to the victims' face. "The gauging of the eyes is certainly a new development."

"Can you determine what instrument was used," Dr. Daniels asked.

"Unfortunately, that has proven difficult," Dr. Brookes replied. He leaned in closer to the body, encouraging the others to follow suit.

"Because of the composition of the eyeball and surrounding flesh, with each stabbing motion, jagged edges were left, thereby rendering a crossing of injuries."

"So there's no clear marks for testing," Detective Phillips' mused.

"Precisely," Dr. Brookes concurred. "Had the entry area been tauter instead of fluid, the demarcations may have been cleaner."

"I don't think it's an intellectual stretch to say the injuries to the eyes are a sign of rage," Dr. Brookes continued. "Of course, I will run fingerprints and complete a dental examination to see if we can identify the victim. But you know how long that can take."

"This may be an indication of the killer losing psychological control," Dr. Daniels suggested. The three attendees turned their focus to the other doctor in the room.

"Nothing else about this murder suggests a loss of control, not physical control. The ligature marks are consistent with the previous ones, the clothing... physically, the killer was able to restrain the victim and dispose of them in much the same way as the previous ones." Dr. Daniels continued. "But, something pushed the killer with this victim and he or she lashed out physically; quite possibly because of a psychological push."

Dr. Brookes walked around the body and looked at it as if seeing it for the first time.

"That leads me to the other marked difference between this murder and the others," Dr. Brookes continued where Dr. Daniels left off. He moved to a table near the front of the room and retrieved an evidence bag. The single black patent leather shoe was clearly visible through the bag.

"The question is where's the other shoe," Dr. Brookes proposed.

"Did the killer forget to put it on," Addison asked.

"Was it lost before the drop site," Detective Phillips suggested.

"Or is there another explanation..." Dr. Daniels added.

Grace worked feverishly at her sewing machine while Madeline St. James cleaned the family home. Grace awoke long before her family, anxious to get the newest outfit underway. She also managed to make a phone call to the international distributor where she purchased her patent leather shoes. Drake's antics from the night before set a fire under Grace. She was disgusted by him and equally disgusted by the black woman currently working in her home. The outfit Grace was currently finalizing was more garish than any of the others. It had nearly every color in the rainbow in horizontal stripes and multicolor polka dots, and an exaggerated collar with bright red trim.

The television mindlessly played in the background. Grace kept up with the news, particularly after her murders were determined to be the work of a serial killer. A serial killer, Grace thought, as the Singer hummed. Grace was mentioned with the likes of Ted Bundy, Charles Manson, Hitler, well known male serial killers. And now Anna Black and Grace Pembroke Wetherby...serial killers...female serial killers... Grace wondered how many women had been given that distinctive labeling. Probably not many, she contended as the news reporter relayed information about Anna Black's capture and pending trial.

Anna was clearly unintelligent as she allowed herself to be caught. Grace thought herself much more astute, more sophisticated than the likes of Anna Black. Anna was, low class, poor white trash. She wasn't cultured and classy like

Grace. Probably grew up on the wrong side of the tracks, close to the niggers, Grace mused, as she completed the last surges to the wide leg pants that tapered unflatteringly at the ankle.

...at least they know her name...

The statement gave Grace pause. She wasn't sure of the voice that spoke those challenging words. Maybe it was Old Man Pembroke. He was always about making a name for yourself and being known for your work. Maybe it was her own ego challenging her anonymity in what would be a legendary scenario. Anna may be ignorant but she garnered great attention. As Old Man Pembroke would say, 'the girl done made a name for herself'. But at what expense, Grace considered. Grace had status in the upper echelons of the community. She was a pillar in her community, known for her charity work and upstanding character. Grace lived in a fine home, had two beautiful children and the semblance of a good marriage. She was famous in her own right. Could she dare risk all that for infamy?

There was a light rap at the door that brought Grace out of her cyclical thinking.

"Yes," she replied, hating the fact she was being disturbed. Instinctively, Grace leaned in front of her sewing machine to hide her current masterpiece.

The door opened and the girl stepped in.

"I've finished with the list you provided," Madeline said.

"Already?"

"Yes," Madeline affirmed.

"I'm sure you couldn't have done a thorough job that quickly," Grace snapped.

"I would be more than happy for you to check my work Mrs. Wetherby," Madeline replied coolly.

"Trust me I will." The outfit wasn't quite finished. This was not part of Grace's meticulous plan. She had to think fast.

"Fine. Go upstairs and round up the clothes from the hampers. I will be with you shortly."

"Yes ma'am," Madeline replied and closed the door.

Grace was not pleased. She turned back to her machine, determined to finish up as quickly as possible. This one was testing her patience. All Grace needed to do was hand sew the last button on the clownish ensemble and the outfit would be complete. In her haste to finish up, Grace inadvertently jabbed the sharp needle into her finger, missing the button hole completely.

"Gottdammit!"

Grace pierced her finger deeply; breaking the seal of the latex gloves she wore. She was bleeding and a drop of blood fell onto the costume in an area obscured by bright colors and patterns. Grace hadn't paid attention as she threw the button across the room, frustrated from being disturbed and now having to rush.

"To hell with it," she said aloud as she scooped up the costume and stormed out of her sewing room. The help should still be upstairs, so getting into the laundry room without being seen shouldn't be a problem. Grace walked speedily through the house, passed the kitchen and into the laundry room. Everything else was already in place. All that was missing was the costume. Grace decided to lay in wait for the girl. That upped the anxiety and excitement level. She was hungry for her next kill. She hoped this one would satiate her completely.

Chapter Twelve

Addison was not looking forward to another session with Anna, but Dr. Daniels felt it necessary. Addison knew Dr. Daniels to be meticulous about her work, leaving no stone unturned. She would not be satisfied until she knew everything there was to know about the angel of death. After processing through the standard search protocols, Dr. Daniels and her assistant were escorted back to the same interview room they used before. Addison considered asking if she could opt out of this particular session but she knew her question would be in vain. Dr. Daniels wanted her there, experientially as well as for a second opinion, firsthand.

Dr. Daniels was relaxed as she sat at the steel table, awaiting her clients' arrival. She learned over the years, that it didn't pay to be anxious in situations like this. Inevitably, a client would pick up on the therapists' heightened energy and utilize it to derail the interviewing process. What Dr. Daniels knew for sure is how well Anna Black could sideswipe an interview. So Chloe focused on her breathing. She wanted to keep a cool head to deal with whatever her client brought to the table.

Addison heard clanking chains nearing the doorway. She braced herself. Unlike her boss, Addison wasn't quite as skilled at keeping her nervousness at bay. When Anna walked in, something was different. Her head was down, she didn't look up. Even after the guards hitched her shackles to the table, Anna never raised her head. Dr. Daniels didn't immediately address her; opting instead to wait and see what Anna would say or do.

Dr. Daniels waited for several minutes. Still nothing. Anna just sat there with her head hung low; her platinum blonde hair shielding her face from view. If this were to continue, Dr. Daniels' time with Anna could end without a word being spoken.

"Anna, do you remember me?"

Dr. Daniels waited to see if she would reply. Just as Chloe was about to address her again, Anna eased her head up. Her eyes were the first thing you could see and they were wild. And then Anna's full face came into view even though she was still looking from under her ragged bangs. The wide toothy smile almost distracted you from how sallow and pale her face was. Dr. Daniels and Addison simultaneously noted the deep, penetrating scratches to Anna's cheeks. One could tell that when the marks were inflicted, they bled, as tinges of crimson still dotted the lines.

"What happened to your face, Anna," Dr. Daniels asked.

Anna's eerie smile never faded and her eyes darted between the doctor and her assistant before she spoke.

"I wanted to feel…"

Addison was immediately taken aback by the inmate's response but Dr. Daniels remained externally unaffected.

"Tell me more, Anna."

"What more is there to say?" Anna's response time was faster but her affect remained the same.

"So you scratched yourself?"

"Isn't that obvious doctor?"

She had a point, Dr. Daniels had to admit.

"So before that, you weren't feeling anything?"

Anna's eyes settled on Dr. Daniels, and then Anna slightly tilted her head, much like a dog when his master is speaking to him.

"I used to cut myself when I was little. That helped me feel. Haven't done that in a while. I never forgot how it felt, though, placing that cool steel blade against my warm flesh, that first piercing pain with my heart beating so fast I thought it would explode out of my chest. The blade slicing through my skin so smooth and even and then the best part, you know what the best part was Dr. Daniels? Finally my hot red blood oozing out...Every part of that process made me feel something...different somethings..." Anna smiled as she reminisced. Her smile was innocent and disarming like a child remembering their fondest toy.

"The last time I really felt anything was when I was in Thomasville, helping those unfortunate souls. That was an awful long time ago; at least it feels like a long time ago. They don't let me around people too much since I've been in here so there was nobody to help and nobody to help me so I helped myself, Dr. Daniels... I helped myself feel..."

Addison scribbled in her notebook trying to take down every word. And then Anna spoke again.

"Enough about me," she began, "I want to talk about someone else."

"Who would you like to talk about," Dr. Daniels asked, her curiosity piqued. She hoped Anna would give her greater insight into a victim, why she chose them, something that would help in building the profile.

"Let's talk about who else is being hunted," Anna continued. She put her bound hands on the table and intertwined her fingers.

"Who would that be," Dr. Daniels asked.

"So what are you all calling her now, the... mmm... the ... oh yeah, the baby doll killer! That's it! The Baby Doll Killer! That's who I want to talk about!"

Dr. Daniels was surprised by the inquiry but paid close attention to what was said.

"You called the killer a she. Anna do you think the baby doll killer is a woman?"

"What kind of doctor are you? Doctors are supposed to be smart and know stuff ordinary people don't. You don't seem very smart today, doctor."

Dr. Daniels didn't reply.

"Of course she's a woman. I mean, who else is going to bother to do half the things she does with all the costuming and make-up? No man has the time or the talent for such things. Besides, if it was a man doing the killing, there'd be a lot more shedding of blood. See, men are violent that way. When they kill, it's reckless and sloppy and they leave lots of clues and blood around. But not this lady. Nope, she's just like me. The people I helped didn't bleed. They went on peacefully to the great beyond. It's a woman doing the helping in that situation."

Admittedly, Dr. Daniels was impressed with Anna's insight. She looked to Addison's reflection in the two-way mirror to ensure she was making notes. The pen in her assistant's hand blazed across the paper.

"Thanks for sharing your thoughts about that situation, Anna," Dr. Daniels commented. "Is it okay if we talk about you now?"

Anna's eyes were still big and wild. She looked as though every eye muscle was being used to maintain her gaze.

"Sure doctor but before we do, I just have one more thing to say about that other lady."

"Okay Anna, what is that?"

"I don't appreciate her being a part of my byline, added to my story like she and I are working for the same great cause. She's a murderer Dr. Daniel's, a murderer. Even though she may not be as messy as a man doing it, it's still murder plain and simple. Do you know why she's killing those people? Huh, Dr. Daniels? Are they sick, and helpless or in a lot of pain longing for relief? Are their days filled with machines and medicines that barely keep them alive? I don't think so. I am a helper, Dr. Daniels. I helped people to escape from pain and suffering. I helped people so they didn't have to be strapped to machines breathing for 'em and needles stuck in their arms and paining them constantly. I helped people. She's killing people. There is a difference. You see? I don't think she should be mentioned in the same breath with me. I helped lots of people, lots of people, Dr. Daniels, some you folks don't even know about. But they know. I know. And I helped them all. What has she done? Killed what, two, three people? And those news people mention her in the same breath as Anna Black like we're equal? We are most certainly not equal. She hasn't helped nearly as many folks as I have. WE are not the same, Dr. Daniels, no ma'am, we are NOT the same..."

Even though Anna ranted, she didn't get out of control like she had before. Her voice may have been slightly elevated, especially when she was making a point, but it was not wanton, uncontrolled rage. Addison relaxed a little with Anna's new disposition.

Dr. Daniels took a moment before responding to Anna. The typical open ended question gave Anna too much latitude to misdirect the interview. Closed ended questions, only led to one or two word answers; not necessarily beneficial in this kind of situation. At this point, Dr. Daniels gained practically nothing as far as additional insight into Anna's criminal behavior. At the same time, Anna did make some interesting comments about the other case. Anna showed the true narcissistic personality traits so typical of a serial killer. Dr. Daniels needed to use that to her advantage.

"Anna, what do you think should happen to someone who hurts people and doesn't help them like you?"

Dr. Daniels knew this line of questioning could potentially be a slippery slope but her clinical instinct suggested the inquiry could be worth it.

"You mean like the baby doll lady killer," Anna replied with disdain in her voice. For the first time since the interview began, Anna sat upright in her seat. Her eyes blazed and narrowed as she leaned in.

"Yes, Anna, like her." Dr. Daniels made mental notes of Anna's posture and words.

"People who hurt people deserve to be hurt..." Anna began, the fire in her eyes intensifying as she spoke. "What you need to find out is her motivation for what she's doing doctor. That would tell you if she's a person that's just hurting people for her own enjoyment or if she feels like she is helping people."

"And if she is hurting people just to be hurting people," Dr. Daniels asked.

"Then she needs to be sent to the pits of a bottomless hell! And it doesn't need to be quick either, doctor. She needs to suffer like she has made those poor people suffer. Yeah, send her back to the gates of hell where her soul came from," Anna replied definitively.

"And if she thinks she's helping people," Dr. Daniels posited.

"Then treat her like she's a helper," Anna replied with just as much conviction as her previous statement.

"And how is that? How do we treat someone who thinks she's a helper but still killed people?"

Anna paused and sat slowly back in her seat. You could almost see the wheels in her mind turning. Addison noted the client's physical manifestations as she sat on the edge of her seat, waiting to hear what Anna said next.

"That is a good question doctor. But it lets me know you don't think I'm very smart."

"Why would you say that?"

"Because, whatever my answer would be, in response to your question about this other person, would be like self-incrimination... You want me to tell you what should happen to me while telling you what should happen to her. Why not just ask instead of dancing around it?"

"Okay, Anna," Dr. Daniels responded. "What do you think should happen to you?"

Anna paused briefly before answering.

"Well, in my way of thinking, I should be allowed to help those who cannot help themselves. That's how I see it. I have saved souls from a sad life. There are so many more people, doctor, who could benefit from my kind of helping. Now, I know you and your little assistant, and the news people and the courts and all those other folks are out there judging me like I have done something wrong, like I'm a bad person. Like I had selfish intentions or bad motives for what I did. You probably want to see ole Anna Black hang or get the poison in the arm! Maybe you want to see Anna in front of a firing squad or something like that," Anna scoffed as she continued.

"But that tells me you all just don't understand. Maybe you don't want to understand that what I have done is a good thing. In order to take a life you have to be living a life. The folks I helped were barely clinging to a painful bit of life. That's why I know what I did was good."

"So in your opinion, you should be set free?"

"I may not be a doctor, or as smart as you Chloe, but I am not an ignorant woman by far," Anna began. The shackles clanked as Anna replaced her chained hands on the metal desk.

"I don't think you're ignorant," Dr. Daniels offered.

Anna calling Dr. Daniels by her first name suggested personal infringement to Dr. Daniels; that the line of questioning may be frustrating the client.

"And please, refer to me as doctor or Dr. Daniels."

Calling the doctor by her first name was a calculated thing for Anna. This wasn't her first time dealing with head doctors. She knew they had buttons that could be pushed too and she intended to push a few of Dr. Daniels.

"Does that bother you doctoorrr? That somebody like me would address you by name instead of title?"

The creepy smile was back. Addison saw the transformation as though it were in slow motion.

The hair on the back of her neck stood on end. Addison crossed and uncrossed her legs. She could feel the tension in the small steel-laden room rising.

Deflection, side stepping, and redirecting. These were the hallmark tools of a narcissistic personality disorder. Dr. Daniels briefly contemplated replying to what she knew was a bait question. Instead, Dr. Daniels folded her hands one over the other and looked at Anna.

Anna was good at the nonverbal, too. She loved the cat and mouse; the dance between herself and whoever underestimated her. Anna hoped the doctor would fall in line and lose focus on her intended direction; playing along with where Anna intended to take her.

"I know you'll never admit it. You are far too professional for that, aren't you, Chloe? But you do; you think I'm dumb, backwoods, ignorant. You have to in order to ask the questions you're asking."

"No, I don't think that at all," Dr. Daniels replied. Chloe's mouth said no but her eyes smiled;

taking a page from Anna's own playbook. The two exchanged a quiet intense moment when no one spoke. They just smiled at each other. Neither was genuine.

Stalemate...

"I do have one last question Anna, if you don't mind," Dr. Daniels began.

"What would that be Dr. Daniels?"

"We haven't talked very much about your family, your sister in particular."

Dr. Daniels waited to see if Anna would have a pronounced reaction or any reaction at all. Addison prayed there would be no escalation. She didn't know if her heart could take another one.

Anna didn't say anything at first. Instead she started to tap her index finger on the table. Her timed hand movement made the chains on her arm rattle. It was the only sound that could be heard in the room. The guard watching through the two-way glass stepped closer. He, like Addison, could sense a shift in the room's energy, even through thick glass.

Everybody watched Anna, not sure what her next move would be. She continued to tap her finger. The chains kept rattling.

"My father is kind but woefully faithful to a woman who is self-centered and not in touch with reality. She creates her own reality and then doesn't like how it looks so she cries a lot about the messes she has made. My sister? Precious little Angel? She was supposed to be the answer to my mother's self-indulgent prayer. I guess one perfect daughter was not enough for her. No. One sweet, loving little girl wasn't enough. She had to go and have another baby. And what did she get? How did the big man in the sky answer her prayer? She got a baby who will always be a baby that will never be able to do anything but eat, shit and cry!"

The finger tapping stopped and the laughing took over. Anna threw her head back and laughed out loud, doubling over; putting her hands against her stomach like the depth of humor made her stomach hurt. It got so good to Anna she repeatedly slapped her hand against the table. Her hand slapped loudly. The chains banged louder.

"Does that answer your question, Dr. Daniels? That's my family in a nutshell," Anna continued to laugh until it faded and then she was solemn again.

"I really wanted to help her," Anna said under her breath.

"I'm sorry Anna, what did you say," Dr. Daniels inquired.

"I said, I really wanted to help her."

"Who?"

"My mommy's little Angel," Anna replied. "She should have been my first..."

Chapter Thirteen

Madeline couldn't wait for her first shift with the Wetherby family to be over. It had been a good day but a long one. She had a big exam coming up and Madeline needed time to study. All she could think about right now was putting in this last load of laundry and getting off her tired feet. Although her compensation package included accommodations in the Wetherby home, Madeline hadn't quite moved her stuff over. She would go home tonight, study in her own place, and sleep in her own bed.

As she carried the laundry bag through the lower level of the home, Madeline looked for Mrs. Wetherby. That woman is a piece of work, Madeline thought as she crossed the kitchen. Madeline only hoped she wouldn't run into her again, and if she absolutely had to, it would be when she was leaving for the evening. Madeline made her way through the kitchen and around the corner to the laundry room. Just one more load to go...

Grace could hear her coming. This was the exciting part, lying in wait. She opted to stand in the small hallway behind the laundry room and sneak up on the girl once she was inside. Grace could hardly contain herself. Adrenaline pumped wildly through her blueblood veins. Madeline's only focus was the washing machine and getting off work. She absentmindedly began loading the washer thinking forward to her evening activities. Madeline started to hum. It was something she did when she worked. Grace made her move, walking on tiptoe so as to not make a sound.

The musical notes were stopped short in Madeline's throat as Grace laced the stocking around her neck and pulled with all her might. Madeline's eyes bulged as she found it difficult to breathe. Instinctively, she wrestled against whatever was holding her. Grace was having a harder time choking this one out. The girl was small physically but she was feisty. A flash of her husband ogling the black bitch sizzled across

Grace's brain. She gritted her teeth and pulled the hose tighter, constantly wrapping the excess around her hands to tighten the noose.

"Die bitch," she whispered through clenched teeth. Grace's thin lips were pulled back as she wrestled to gain control of his husband's latest desire. Madeline's eyes bulged as she heard the words of her attacker. Madeline tried not to panic but it was getting more difficult. Her vision started to blur as oxygen failed to reach her brain. Madeline fought to stay focused, to find a way out of this. She closed her eyes. Trying to get her fingers between the thing tightening on her neck. It wasn't working. Madeline threw her elbow back, connecting with Grace's gut.

"Ugh!" Grace was caught completely off guard and her hold on the pantyhose loosened. Madeline felt the connection ease and relished a less constrained breath of air. Now she was the one growling trying to wrestle herself free.

"Grr...."

Grace refused to be defeated by the likes of Mad-e-line or whoever the hell she was. This girl represented all of them; all the help her lousy husband lusted for and even the one she lost. Grace fought to regain the upper hand. The two tussled. Clothes from the laundry basket spilled onto the floor. Madeline tried to get herself turned around to face her attacker. Grace started to lose her footing, slipping on the dirty clothes. Madeline felt the shift and attempted to capitalize on it. But Grace was fueled by anger. She quickly overpowered Madeline whose sole source of fuel was fear. Using everything within arm's reach to her greatest advantage, Grace found the open door of the washing machine and bashed it into Madeline wherever the strike would land. The blow landed in the center of Madeline's back and she fell forward. Grace lost total grip of the hose. When Madeline went flailing, Grace took the opportunity to go after her; grabbing Madeline by her curly hair and spinning her around. Madeline screamed out in pain.

"Shut up you cunt nigger," Grace yelled back; unconcerned with the ruckus in the laundry room potentially waking up her sleeping family upstairs.

Grace held tightly to Madeline's hair with one gloved hand, despising the touch and feel of it even through latex. With her other hand, Grace grabbed the washing machine door and used it like a ramming rod - once, twice, three times against the crown of the girls' head. Blurred vision returned, but this time for a different reason. Madeline swung her arms wildly trying to interfere with what was hurting her head. But just like the cartoon short guy trying to box a giant, her arm throws no longer connected.

Grace felt deep seated satisfaction as she whammed the washer door against the girl's head. Every thud was like music to her ears. And when the little nigger girl screamed or moaned? It fueled the sadistic part of Grace's otherwise lily-white soul. She grunted with every blow. "Mmm... mmm...mmm..."

And then there was a different kind of thud and Madeline's' screams became moans. Grace reacted to splatters of wetness on her skin before her mind comprehended what her eyes saw. However, that didn't stop Grace from forcefully swinging the washing machine door, over and over and over. Grace was in a fury and the softening thuds against the girls' skull paled in comparison to the ruckus of bravado in her own. She scarcely paid attention to the heaviness of the head she was holding as Madeline's lifeless body hung suspended by Grace's tight grip of her hair.

Grace was near exhaustion as she swung the door one last time, simultaneously releasing the heaviness that was in her other hand. She allowed her legs to slip from under her and she plopped to the floor. Her breathing was labored and every exposed part of her body was thickly sticky. The house was quiet again. The only thing that could be heard was Grace's panting. And then she too fell silent. It was like Grace was coming off a drug induced state. Her eyes widened as she looked around the laundry room. Her mind finally registered the scarlet redness splattered on the walls, the floor, the laundry basket, the dirty clothes. Then, as if she saw them for the first time,

Grace looked at her hands. She turned both hands over slowly and stared at them. Grace shook her hands in the air as if that would somehow remove the stains. It didn't. Pushing herself up from the floor, Grace wiped her gloved, blood stained hands on her pants. She scowled as she looked at the heap of girl crumpled on the floor.

"You made a mess, tramp..."

Detective Phillips and Dr. Daniels sat uncomfortably in the two wooden chairs immediately in front of the chief's desk. Sitting there was much like being in the principal's office when you knew you were in trouble. The chief was pacing back and forth; running his hands over his nearly bald head. Dr. Daniels and Phillips watched; their eyes moving back and forth as he paced. No one spoke. It wasn't safe.

When the chief finally sat down, the look on his face said it all.

"I just got off a 40-minute phone call with the new prosecutor, Judith M. Norwood."

Phillips slid slightly down in his seat. He was not a fan. When the chief eye-balled him disapprovingly, Phillips slid back to an upright position.

"To say that one minute on the phone with that woman is more than enough... do I even need to say what 40 minutes was like?"

There was no verbal response. It still wasn't safe to speak.

"I think she has forgotten who she works for."

Chloe decided to be brave.

"What do you mean, chief?"

"That... woman, is picking our case apart! I expect that from the defense attorney but not from our own representative!"

Chief Livingston buried his face in his hands. He could feel his pressure rising. Reaching in his top left drawer, he pulled out his bottle of prescription medication and dry swallowed a blood pressure pill.

"I don't care what you two have to do, but you will get this woman off my back. Don't sleep, don't eat if it distracts you from firming up this case. Do not leave a stone unturned. Make it happen! Have I made myself clear?"

Detective Phillips responded with a "yes sir."

Dr. Daniels nodded to the chief as she lifted herself from the horribly uncomfortable chair and made her way to the door. Phillips met her there and opened it for her, like a perfect gentleman. The two walked down the hall; passed the bullpen where other officers were hard at work. They stopped shortly before reaching the elevators.

"Maybe instead of working separately, we need to literally put our heads together, work together in the same space on this thing," Michael suggested.

Equally as frustrated with the lack of progress, Dr. Daniels was amenable to the idea.

"Just tell me where and when."

"Is it okay if I call you later to talk about it?"

"Sure," Chloe responded.

Dr. Daniels made her way to the elevator and Detective Phillips walked with her. He pushed the button and the two waited quietly for the elevator to arrive. Michael stole a glance, always appreciative of Chloe's effortless beauty. Her ensembles were always understated; never flashy, but boy could she turn a head. When Chloe caught him checking her out, she blushed. The ding from the arriving elevator saved Michael from a more embarrassing moment. Stepping to the side, Detective Phillips extended his arm when the doors opened, ushering Dr. Daniels in.

"Call you later," he called after. Chloe smiled as the doors closed.

Chapter Fourteen

This was the first time Grace drew blood. This was the first time her murderous plot didn't go precisely as planned. She had a mess to clean up but there was a problem. Should she clean up first and then go and dump the body or do things the other way around? Clean up would take a while, especially if the laundry room was to be returned to its pristine condition pre-bloodletting. However, if she cleaned first, that meant she could potentially face greater risk of the sun coming up and increased traffic, causing problems with the dumping.

For the first time since Grace decided to be judge, jury and executioner, she started to freak out. First things first, Grace thought as the stickiness on her gloved hands began to congeal. She walked out of the laundry room and down the hall to the half bath; leaving a trail of bloody footprints behind her. The door to the bathroom was closed. It was her own fault. Grace insisted that no bathroom doors ever remain open. She thought it uncouth.

"Dammit," she grunted. Using the tail of her shirt, Grace turned the knob, again leaving traces of the girls' blood on the stainless steel. Flipping the switch for the lights, again, bloody traces were left from the tail of her shirt. Grace crossed the small but well-appointed bathroom and used her shirt once more to turn on the faucet. Grace let the water run until it was near scalding. The hot water began to erase the crime from her gloved hands. Trails of black girl blood commingled with the hot water and Grace watched it swirl down the drain. Once the gloves were nearly clean, Grace removed them and allowed the scalding water to wash over her hands. Physically, her hands weren't bloody, but symbolically, Grace needed them to be clean as well. She started to feel some better as her pale white skin flushed with color from the heat.

And then she looked up into the gold gilded mirror over the basin. Grace's mouth fell open as she saw herself. She was immediately transfixed by the reflection in the mirror. Grace didn't immediately take it as her own. Her strawberry blonde hair was wild and unkempt. Her face was dotted with scarlet spots, smeared by tears she apparently shed. Grace's eyes were wide; not from what she saw but what she'd done.

"Ahh!" Grace exclaimed; having forgotten her hands under the scorching water. Recovering from the sting, Grace turned on the cold water to warm what was already flowing. She pooled the warmer water in her hands and rinsed her face, absolving her skin of the bloody traces. She started to feel better, cleaner. Grace grabbed a small towel and pat dried her face. Never wipe, she thought, it causes premature wrinkling. After smoothing down her hair and coiling it tightly into a bun atop her head, Grace turned off the water, wiped the sink clean, thoughtlessly turned off the light switch and exited the bathroom, closing the door behind her.

Feeling refreshed, at least to some degree, Grace contemplated her next move. She still hadn't fully decided what would be the best next step; the right thing to do given the impending circumstances. An easy solution would be to close the laundry door and hope her family exited for the next school and work day with no need to enter. If she was there, she could monitor their activity and keep them away.

What time is it, she thought. She didn't have on any jewelry so she moved to the kitchen to find the nearest clock. 10:00 p.m. the clock read. She looked at it in disbelief. Where had the time gone? It had never taken her that long to off one before. Had she fallen asleep from exhaustion? Grace wasn't sure. But this whole thing was off. Those feelings of trepidation crept up again. Grace had to make her move and soon.

Grace had been moving around in the dark. She knew her home like the back of her hand so lights in the corridors was unnecessary. Grace didn't see the trail of stains she left on the travertine floors as she walked back down the corridor and re-entered the laundry room. The light was on in there and the mess that lie before her could not be denied. She would have to do something; at least a little something before striking out with the body. That's the decision she made. She would use the cover of darkness to dispose of the trash, get back home, clean herself up, and hopefully get some sleep before time to get her family out of the house the next morning. Then, after the house was cleared, she would attend to the mess in the laundry.

So that's exactly what Grace set out to do. She found an unused pair of rubber gloves in the box above the washer and put them on. The first thing she did was pick up the mess of clothes on the floor. Grace picked the clothing up and tossed it into the still open washer door. She noted the blood pooling on the door and figured it would wash away as the clothes spun. There were a few pieces of dirty clothing under the girl. Grace bent her knees and pushed the body out of the way, wincing all the while, as she retrieved her family's belongings. These particular pieces were soaked in blood. Ordinarily, Grace would require the help to presoak and hand wash such thoroughly soiled items but there was no time for that. Besides, the help lay dead on the floor. She threw them in with the rest of the wash. If she had to run the cycle multiple times to get the clothes clean she would. If not, she would throw them out with the next day's garbage.

With the other bodies, Grace was able to drag them down the hallway with no concern of leavings. This time it was different. This bitch bled, and inevitably trails would be left. Think Gracie Think, she commanded herself as she stood there frowning at the dead bitch that caused all her problems. Sheets!! Sheets! Or garbage bags... Grace was aggravated by her indecisiveness and the quandaries.

"Make A Fucking Decision Already!" Grace instantly covered her mouth. The house was quiet. She needed it to remain that way. She listened for a minute to see if her outburst caused an awakening. The seconds passed slowly as she listened intently. The house remained quiet. Grace breathed a sigh of relief. But she still hadn't decided how best to handle the situation. There were no sheets amongst the items in the laundry so she would have to quietly go to the linen closet on the second floor, retrieve them, and come back downstairs, all without disturbing the house.

Think...

Guest room! She could take the sheets from the guest room bed and use them. No one used that room and they would have no cause to go in there. That was a good solution, Grace thought as she exited the current room and meandered through the hallways to get to the downstairs guest room. Her shoes left less trails this time...

Grace quickly threw the duvet off the queen-sized bed and snatched up the sheets. She was feeling much more optimistic now that at least a fragmented portion of a plan was coming together. Grace needed things to be organized, neat and tidy. Unexplained occurrences and things out of order frayed her nerves, unless, of course, she caused the disorder. Then it was calculated and not happenstance. Like when she set up the help to take the fall for her misdeeds when she was a child. That was calculated and methodical. She thought of her girl, the one she lost and still longed for and still hated for leaving her, as she made her way through the kitchen to pick up garbage bags.

Making her way back to her destination, Grace was winded. She was still a long way away from being done, though. Grace spread out the bedsheets one on top of the other, covering the washroom floor. Stepping on top of the sheets, Grace evaluated the two trash bags she had in her hand against the lump of dead weight splayed on the floor. Grace wasn't sure the girl would fit but what choice did she really have at this point?

Fuck! She thought to herself. In all the skirmish and the messiness of the kill, she still hadn't dressed the girl in the custom costume she made for her. She hadn't made up the girls face or anything. This kill was nothing like the ones before. If there was no semblance to the others, Grace wouldn't get the credit she deserved for taking out another worthless coon. Grace needed the credit. It's part of what made her tick. The costume had to be put on. She'd worked too hard on this one.

Fortunately, the outfit hadn't gotten mussed. Grace put it up on one of the shelves so the girl wouldn't see it upon entering. She retrieved it, stepping over the body as she did. Grace despised the undressing and redressing part. Being that close and actually touching the skin of a person she really considered more of a thing always repulsed her. But she had to go through that part to get to the best part... the humiliation. And when the bodies were found, the public humiliation. So Grace sucked it up, and began undressing her latest victim. She would need an extra trash bag to dispose of the girls' belongings. She made a mental note to retrieve one.

The girl's clothes were sticking to her black body because of all the blood. Even against the girls' darker skin, the now maroon coagulated blood stains stood out. It would certainly come through on the fabric of her costume. The next girl would have to be quick and far less sloppy.

Grace managed to get the girls work shoes off and her black work pants. She noted the frilly pink lace panties the girl wore. Probably a knock-off from Walmart, Grace thought. She had a smirk on her face, regaled by her own humor.

"Harlot," she spat at the one who could no longer hear.

Grace's mind went back to the previous night. Her husband's disgusting display of self-satisfaction, knowing full well, he was jacking off to thoughts of this thing. Grace handled the girl rougher after that disturbing memory. Getting her shirt off was harder. The once dingy white button down was now soaked through. The latex gloves Grace wore were covered with the girls' secretions as well. Finally, the undressing was over and a devilish grin replaced the frown Grace wore.

Taking more time than she had with the disrobing, Grace gently laid the colorful costume on the sheets that still remained clean. She admired her work; running her gloved hands over the fabric. Her smile broadened. This was by far one of the highlights of the whole murderous process. Grace had done exceptional work with this costume and the colors would certainly pop when the girls' body was eventually found. Grace got the pants on easy enough, but then she remembered. The buttons on the top were a mock opening. The top didn't really unbutton. She would have to put the costume over the girls' head in order to fully dress her.

Grace stomped her feet like a bratty two-year-old. She was aggravated. Time was ticking by and she knew it.

"Grrrr," she grunted and exhaled.

She really didn't want to touch the girl more than necessary. And her face, well, her entire head, was gross. Grace got back down on her knees straddling the body. This close, Grace could really see up close, the damage the machine door caused.

"Had you simply cooperated, none of this messiness would have had to happen," Grace said, chastising the deceased.

"You brought this on yourself..."

The head was heavy; weightier than Grace remembered when she wielded it recklessly against the washer door. It was difficult to balance pulling the shirt over it. Grace bunched up the shirt, bunching the tail to the neckline. Then, holding the shirt with one hand, she grabbed the head with the other and placed the shirt over. There was a distinct thud as Grace allowed the head to drop. This body sat longer than the others so the arms were harder to bend and move. Grace worked up a sweat as she threaded one and then the other arm into the once vibrant top.

Once Grace got the shirt completely on, she looked down with dissatisfaction. Her hard work was nearly ruined with the bloody smudges darkening the once brilliant colors.

"You ruined it you trashy bitch!"

The culmination of all the day's aggravating moments rained down on Grace at once. She hated herself because she was on the verge of tears. Crying was for weaklings and Old Man Pembroke never tolerated tears, not even when Grace's mother died. But here she was sitting on top of a dead black girl with hot tears dripping from her weary eyes. Without additional provocation, Grace started beating on the dead girls' chest, pouring out pinned up feelings of past and present hurts she was too dignified to give voice to. With every wail of her fist, the tears continued to fall, hotter and faster.

Grace was tired; tired of pretending that her high profile life was perfect, that her husband was loyal and that her children loved her without condition. None of that was true. Grace's life, although affluent was far from perfect. And her husband? That shell of a man? He was loathsome at best. Grace desperately wanted to believe that her precious children, the one's she sacrificed her petite figure for, really loved her. But she saw how they responded to the help; whether they'd known them one day or a dozen. They showed the help affection, genuine affection. They liked the help more than they liked her. Much like she loved her girl more than her own mother...

Grace sobbed a while longer, allowing herself the indulgence of a brief pity party. She consoled herself and eventually, got on with the task at hand. Grace lifted herself from atop the body and grabbed the trash bags. She managed to get one over the head and down to the girls' waist. Before bagging the rest of her, Grace put on the frilly lace socks. Then she moved to the shelf, retrieved the patent leather shoes, and placed them on the girls' feet. They were nearly a perfect fit; as though she'd measured the girl before putting them on. Once that was accomplished, Grace repositioned herself behind the girl so she could roll her onto the sheet. But the sheets were not cooperative and neither was the dead one. Grace pushed. At first, the body didn't move. She needed leverage. Grace pushed again; this time putting her legs into it. Finally, the body started to go in the right direction, but the trash bags were too slick and the sheets were pushed as well.

Grace pushed the hair out of her face that had fallen from her tight bun. Once again it was necessary for Grace to lift the heavy body onto the sheet. That proved nearly impossible with the trash bag on. She had to undo what she'd just done. Tears welled up in Grace's eyes again. Once the bag was removed, Grace grabbed the stiffened arms and lifted the body, turning it onto the sheet. It took several lifts and some dragging, with her feet firmly planted on the sheet in order to get the body in the right position.

If giving up was an option, at this point Grace certainly would have. She was exhausted. She kept telling herself repeatedly how she wasn't a quitter, she had to finish what she started, how time was running out. Grace managed to get the sheet back over the girls' head with the same energy required the first time. Finally, the body was wrapped up. All that was left was getting the body in the car, making the drop, keeping her family away from the laundry and then clean up. Yeah, Grace could see the finish line, but it still seemed so very far away.

Chapter Fifteen

Chloe couldn't believe she was making such a fuss over what to wear. She and Detective Phillips agreed to meet at her place in an hour and here she stood, in front of the full-length mirror in her bedroom trying to figure out what to put on. He would expect her to be professional, because of the nature of the meeting. Yet, this was after hours in her home. Certainly, casual would be the way to go. But just how casual?

Chloe tried on a pair of jeans. Too tight. Then another pair. Uncomfortable. She did have her 'go to' pair of jeans, every woman does, but that pair? Grace laughed at herself for making such a fuss. This was a work date, well, not a date. This was work. Walking back to her closet, Chloe grabbed a tee shirt and threw on her comfy jeans, even though she had snags and rips in them, and closed the closet doors. No more fussing over clothes.

Addison was working in the office when Chloe emerged.

"I've organized the Black files in reverse date order. They are stacked here. I've also organized the transcripts from the interviews and placed them here in the center. In the event there's additional time or need for cross reference, I've also placed the files on the doll killer in this stack."

"Thanks, Addison, appreciate that."

Dr. Daniels set to work. It would be good to focus on something other than her attire; help the time until his arrival pass more quickly. Addison dug right in next to her, reviewing the earlier files on the Anna Black case. Not long after, the doorbell rang. Surprisingly, Chloe felt her pulse increase. That never happened before when it came to Detective Phillips or maybe, she just never paid any attention.

Either way, she was glad Addison responded to the door and she didn't have to. Chloe would have a moment to pull herself together and prepare for a work session. A work session, she reminded herself.

"Good evening," Detective Phillips said as he entered the office.

Chloe looked up from her position on the floor. He smiled as their eyes met.

"Good evening Detective," she began.

He cut her off mid salutation.

"Please, I am in your home. Call me Michael."

She nodded and accepted the pleasant chastisement. He smiled down at her. Addison stood slightly behind him noting the interchange.

"Oh, I almost forgot," Michael said. He lifted a bottle of white wine from the burlap bag in his hand.

"I'll take care of that," Addison replied, accepting the bottle as Michael turned in her direction. She reached for the bag as well, and Michael smiled as he handed it to her.

"Thanks Addison."

"You're welcome."

Addison disappeared down the hall and into the kitchen. Chloe extended her hand offering Michael a seat on the couch. He declined and positioned himself across the cocktail table from her on the floor.

"Addison was kind enough to organize the work," Chloe began, explaining the various stacks on the table.

"Where do you suggest we start?" Michael inquired.

"At the beginning," Chloe replied with a sigh.

They each grabbed one of the files from the stack that was in reverse chronological order and opened it. Addison came back and positioned herself at the 'head' of the table, on the shortest end between the two of them. Each of them dug in to the files. Michael asked for some scratch paper to jot notes and Addison readily obliged as she pre-prepared with a stack of it at the ready.

Michael looked over at Chloe. He thought he was being discreet, peering over the top of the open file. He couldn't help himself. Seeing her in her own environment, relaxed but still so beautiful. He loved the way she mussed her hair and pushed up on her reading glasses as she concentrated. He returned to his file, hoping his stares went unnoticed. For Chloe they did, as she was dug in, reviewing some of the initial deaths attributed to Anna Black. But Addison saw him. She always had a feeling there was an unspoken or even unacknowledged chemistry between the two. Michael was making his attraction obvious.

The three worked in silence for quite a while. The silence was broken by a churning from someone's stomach. They each looked up from what they were doing.

"It wasn't me," Addison suggested.

"Me either," Michael quickly chimed in.

Chloe looked up embarrassed.

"Well..." she began, intending to defend herself. She was busted and the other two laughed at her expense. Chloe covered her face with the manila folder.

"Don't," Michael said, reaching across the table and lowering the file. The smile from his face lessened but the intensity in his eyes grew.

"Don't what," Chloe asked more coyly than she intended.

"Don't ever hide that beautiful face."

Chloe felt her cheeks grow warm and now she desperately wanted to cover her face to shield herself from blushing in front of him. Michael didn't drop his gaze. The intensity between the two was electric. Addison felt her own cheeks warm.

"I'll get the take out menus," Addison offered, excusing herself from the table.

Chloe didn't know what to say. She couldn't stop smiling and that made the situation more awkward for her. It wasn't that Chloe didn't get attention from men. It had been a long time since she allowed it to affect her in this way.

"Detective Phillips, you are embarrassing me," Chloe said, still finding it hard to erase the smile from her lips.

"Detective, okay," Michael laughed. "But every word of it is true."

Michael wasn't sure why he felt so emboldened. He'd admired Chloe for a long time. Maybe she needed to get a sense of what he really thought about her.

"Back to work detective."

"Yes ma'am."

He was smiling, too.

Addison returned to the office with menus in hand. The group settled on Thai and Addison ordered for everyone. They all went back to working on their files and discussing some of the histories while they waited for dinner to arrive. The conversation was professional enough, but the undercurrent of sexualized tension between Michael and Chloe could not be ignored.

For the first time, Addison felt like a third wheel. She was relieved when the phone rang and she could excuse herself from the room. Addison fully expected it to be confirmation that their order was in route. Surprisingly, the call came from the prosecutor's office. When Addison re-entered the office, she had an announcement to make.

"Anna Black has decided to testify."

Chapter Sixteen

To say Grace was exhausted was an understatement. She was physically and mentally spent. But there were still things she had to accomplish. First things first, though. Grace opened the door to the laundry room and peeked her head out to make sure the coast was clear. She looked down one way and then the other before turning around to retrieve the body. Grace used a bit of ingenuity. Instead of wrapping the sheets around the body, she decided to use the sheets as a means of transporting the girl down to the car. The body was heavy; heavier it seemed since it was stiffening. Grace put her back into it and pulled. She managed to finagle the body around the corners and doorway of the washroom. The hallway was a breeze, as there were no obstructions she had to contend with.

Grace did have to turn a few corners in moving the body from the kitchen to the garage. In her haste to rid herself of this part of the job, Grace pulled with added force and there was an unexpected thud. She halted her forward motion to see what happened. When she realized the dead girl's head hit the bottom of the door jam, Grace snickered.

"...serves you right Black bitch..."

Grace's snicker turned into a heartier laugh as she continued to pull the girl the remaining few feet to the door. She was virtually delirious. Grace didn't recognize it in herself. Grace allowed enough space for the kitchen door to open. She backed through it pulling the load in front of her. Thud, thud, thud... Grace dragged the body down the steps and onto the concrete garage floor. Releasing the sheets, Grace stood up and put her hand on the small of her back. She was achy from all the manual labor. Grace reached inside the van and released the switch that caused the automatic side door to slide back. Wiping her forehead with the back of her hand. Grace bent over again, this time with the intention of lifting one part of the wrapped body into the truck and then the other.

Grace failed to bend her knees when she went to lift the sheet and instead of gaining any headway, she ended up pulling in vain. Her level of aggravation began to rise again as she reached for the sheet with vigor.

Grace sounded like an animal as she did what she should have done the first time – bent her knees and put her back into it. She managed to get one end up and systematically pulled and lifted it into the van's bed. Grace had to use her arms to steady the portion she had inside as it immediately started to slip. Lifting a bit more of the body in, more from the middle, she was able to steady it enough to shimmy her way down to the other end; bracing the head against the back wall of the van. One more dead lift and Grace cleared the floor and the lip of the van. Grace shifted her weight and turned on her heels, enabling herself to push the bag in the rest of the way.

"Whew..."

She stopped just long enough to catch her breath. Mentally checking loading the body of her checklist, Grace re-entered the kitchen, crossed to the washroom where she discarded the soiled latex gloves and closed the door. On her way back out of the house, Grace grabbed her purse and car keys. She closed the kitchen door behind her. All she could hope was that her lush of a husband drunk enough to be sound asleep and her children were so lost in dream land that the sound of the garage door opening didn't wake them.

Grace fired up the ignition and the dashboard came to life. As she turned on the headlights, her eyes immediately went to the LED clock. It read 12:30 a.m. Grace blew out hard, causing her cheeks to puff as she did. One thing at a time Gracey girl, one thing at a time, she thought to herself as she put the van in gear and backed out of the garage. Grace's thoughts were less of her slumbering family as they were of where to take the garbage, as she hit the remote to close the garage door.

She didn't have a lot of time to drive aimlessly around in search of the perfect spot. Grace knew this time the dump site would have to be closer to her home than she would like. She really wanted to thoroughly clean before it was time for her family to wake up. Grace drove out of her subdivision and headed for the interstate, determined to figure it out by the time she got to the highway. As she drove down her tree lined street, Grace was temporarily blinded by oncoming headlights. As the car neared her, Grace habitually looked over to see who was in the passing car. She quickly turned her eyes straight ahead, having recognized her neighbor from a few houses down.

Dammit... I know he saw me... he knows me... he knows my van...dammit!

Theirs was a close-knit neighborhood in as much as an exclusive gated community could be. Yes, he saw her, but she also saw him. What the hell was he doing coming in this time of night, Grace thought. She put on her blinker to turn onto the adjoining street. Ordinarily, this was the highlight for Grace. The undeniable heavy pounding of her heart, the quickening of her pulse, the built-in risk of getting caught all added to the culmination of her work. Seeing the neighbor, added to the risk and the thrill.

Graced moved down the quiet side streets until she came to the first four way stop; signifying her exit from the suburbs and into Atlanta proper. In less than ten miles Grace would be at the apex of the interstate connectors where highways 85, 75 and 20 all crossed paths. Traffic thickened as Grace made her way toward the interstate. Third shifters were feigning off sleep as they made their way to and from work. They all converged at the entrances and exits of the interstate. They all stood in Grace's way.

Although not ordinarily prone to road rage, the elapsing time and the tasks that lie before her caused Grace to be a little more on edge than she ordinarily would be. Once she successfully navigated onto the highway and decided on a destination, Grace dipped and swerved through traffic focused on her next step. Grace was eager to check off the next box on her to-do list and the people driving around her were in her way.

"Move it, you fucking moron!" She yelled as she swerved in front of the car driving a speed not to her liking. Grace's face could be paralleled with that of the infamous Cruella de Vill; eyes wide and flaming, teeth drawn back in a sneer. She was on a mission and in her mind, the mission was clear. The faster she dumped the hussy bundled up on her van's floor, the faster she could get back home to take care of her family and plan her next murder.

Grace knew the highway well and knew there would soon be an overpass up ahead. She grinned wider as she eyed her destination. So focused on what was in front of her, she failed to see the car beside her easing into her lane. When Grace finally caught sight of the car in her periphery, she pulled the steering wheel hard and blared on the horn, missing the intruding car by inches. Fortunately, Grace was in the far right lane and there wasn't another car on the right side of her or she would have hit it. Unfortunately, Grace overshot the lane and ended up riding on the raised grid that signified being off road.

The raised grid caused the van to shake robustly. As Grace attempted to move the car back into her lane, she heard what sounded like a pop.

Grace checked her rearview mirror to see if she maybe lost a hubcap. Even though there were lights behind her from oncoming cars, it was still too dark out to tell if she had lost one. Once back in her lane, there weren't any more weird noises so Grace settled back into her seat and focused on reaching the overpass.

More and more cars surrounded her and before long. Grace reduced her speed as traffic slowed. Grace could only see red tail lights in front of her. Traffic jam...

This was not what Grace needed. Was there an accident up ahead? The LED clock blared a bright red 12:59 a.m., mimicking the sea of red that lie before her. When Grace's car came to a complete stop, she dropped her head back onto the headrest.

"What else could possibly go wrong?"

A question, she knew better than to ask, but she raised the question out loud anyway. Her first impulse was to throw the car in park, move to the back of the van and beat the shit out of the trollop that caused all these problems. But all Grace could muster were a few foul words and a few fist pounds to the steering wheel.

Horns blared in the distance as other flustered drivers expressed their exacerbation. Grace's patience had nearly run out and now she was moving at a speed that barely registered on the speedometer. She was so close to the overpass. But with the high volume of traffic, there was no way she could dump the body without being seen. It was too great a risk. She would have to wait until traffic began to move again at a steadier rate and move further down the interstate when traffic thinned out.

Despite the reason why, traffic was not moving to Grace's liking. Her timeframe was all off and now she had to divert from her plan once again to make it all work. Right passed the overpass was an exit that would take her off the highway. If she could just get to that exit, she could dump the body on a side street and re-enter the highway going the opposite direction where traffic was far less congested. Okay. She had a plan.

Traffic picked up a bit and the green and white sign signaling the exit came into view. As she moved slowly under the overpass, Grace looked at the darkened roadside where she would have loved to rid herself of the body had traffic not been an issue. But it was, so Grace didn't allow her mind to linger on what could have been. Maybe this snag in her plan could actually work to her benefit. They would expect to find the next body in the same kind of location where they discovered the others. Dumping on a side street could certainly throw the police and the media off her trail. Grace put on her blinker as she neared the exit for Ralph David Abernathy Ave.

This could be perfect. Black trash dumped on a historically named street in a less than desirable black neighborhood? Yes, this could certainly work to her advantage. This was payback for not being able to dump by MLK. The frown of frustration dissolved and a snide grin invaded Grace's pale face. They killed each other all the time. What difference would one more body make in a place like this?

The sound from the blinker faded as Grace navigated off the interstate toward the street. And then, without warning, the van started to lumber along. Something was wrong... something was terribly wrong...

The End... well, not really

Stay tuned for Mischief's Mayhem

The Third Installment in the Chloe

Daniels Mysteries!

www.ingramcontent.com/pod-product-compliance
Lightning Source LLC
Chambersburg PA
CBHW061001280326
41935CB00009B/789